Praise for *Beating the Deal Killers*

"If you're in the business of selling, make it your business to read this book."

—Andrew Hersam
New York Advertising Director
Sports Illustrated

"To dramatically increase the effectiveness of your sales organization, I highly recommend this book."

—David House
President, Global ES & TCG
American Express

"I've worked with Steve for many years. His voice, his energy, his humor, and his insights are alive and well in this book."

—Edward F. Kelly
President and CEO
American Express Publishing

BEATING THE DEAL KILLERS

Overcoming Murphy's Law
(and Other Selling Nightmares)

STEPHEN A. GIGLIO

McGraw-Hill

New York   Chicago   San Francisco   Lisbon   London
Madrid   Mexico City   Milan   New Delhi   San Juan
Seoul   Singapore   Sydney   Toronto

The *McGraw·Hill* Companies

My messages in this book are dedicated to my mother for instilling courage in me and forever encouraging my sense of humor; to my father for teaching me the miracle of humanity and life and the importance of doing my best; and to my beautiful wife, Ellen, for teaching me the greatest of life's lessons, gratitude and love.

Library of Congress Cataloging-in-Publication Data

Giglio, Stephen A.
    Beating the Deal Killers / Stephen A. Giglio.
        p. cm.
    ISBN 0-07-138551-7 (alk. paper)
    1. Selling.   2. Murphy's law.   I. Title.
HF5438.25 .G535   2002
658.85—dc21

2002008207

1 2 3 4 5 6 7 8 9 0   DOC/DOC   0 9 8 7 6 5 4 3 2

ISBN 0-07-138551-7

McGraw-Hill books are available at special quantity discounts to use as premiums and sales promotions, or for use in corporate training programs. For more information, please write to the Director of Special Sales, Professional Publishing, McGraw-Hill, Two Penn Plaza, New York, NY 10121-2298. Or contact your local bookstore.

This book is printed on recycled, acid-free paper
containing a minimum of 50% recycled, de-inked fiber.

CONTENTS

ACKNOWLEDGMENTS

Writing one's first book is a daunting task. As the beautiful song goes, "You gotta have friends." Here are mine, to be heartily acknowledged for their support and encouragement.

To John Morse, my alter ego, thank you from the bottom of my heart for your honesty, guidance, project management, and dedication to ensuring that this book was written properly and eloquently.

An idea that turned into a book would have gone nowhere without an effective agent. My thanks to Carla Glasser for her immediate and evergreen belief in my message. Step number two of producing a book moves to one's editor. Thank you Susan Clarey for making the idea and book real. My gratitude to Barry Neville for his acceptance of my vision and his 24/7 guidance.

Throughout my years of consulting, several clients and friends have always been there for me, in their support of my work and in their friendship: To Jim Berrien, president of the Forbes Magazine Group, for his ability to keep me challenging myself as a sales and management coach; Tom Ryder, CEO of *Reader's Digest*, for his forever vision of bringing respect back to the profession of selling; David House, president of American Express Global Establishment Services, for his trust in my leadership and introduction into the international arena of salespeople; and to Louis Vlahakes, for his watchful eye over my career. And to The Hunt Club, for ensuring that I am the man I always wanted to be.

Stephen A. Giglio

INTRODUCTION

A merica's economy is dominated by the service sector. Two-thirds of the gross national product is based on consumer spending. It's an industrial base built on a host of people-to-people resources—consumer relations, communications, advertising, product placement, promotion—but, in particular, it's about sales.

Yet, despite the critical role of sales, many salespeople never make the most of their talents. Instead, each time they go out to make a sale, they grit their teeth and hope for the best. Trust me, that won't do.

During my career as a sales and management consultant, I've counseled more than 30,000 people from companies large and small, including some of the finest, best-known corporations in the world. Most are staffed with people who are adept and creative but who too often fail to embrace their responsibilities as salespeople. These are people who are, unfortunately, unwilling or unable to go for it.

Why? Again and again, the problem can be traced to a fear of making a mistake. People are afraid of the deal killers and Murphy's law.

Usually this fear is rooted in false notions, a lack of understanding of the very basics of what makes for successful sales.

In this book, you'll learn how to beat the deal killers and Murphy's law, get the training you need to fight his attacks, and make the sale.

HOW'S YOUR BEDSIDE MANNER?

Some people assume there's got to be a secret system to getting it right every time—a set of tricks. How else, you may ask yourself, can people less competent than I consistently rack up the sales? Forget the temptation to look for a quick and easy answer. Realize from the outset that there's no trick, no secret, no magic bullet.

To make sales—to beat Murphy—you must understand a few simple, but crucial rules of the game. But, if you learn nothing else from this book, if you read no further, please remember this one overriding rule: *Listen before you speak.*

I know what you're thinking, "That's the oldest saw in the book." Sorry, but sometimes old saws stick around because they are so true. This is one of them.

It's important to listen. This is easy to say, but a lot more difficult to do, especially on a regular basis. Listening requires the discipline to learn about your clients ahead of time. This lets you be prepared when the time comes to answer those needs, which is important because (hello, Sales 101) fulfilling clients' needs is the heart of sales. Even if there's not a lot of time for early discovery, you must initiate the listening process from the earliest possible moment.

How do you become a good listener? You must know what to ask. As Sir Francis Bacon said, "Knowledge is power." The more you know about the needs of your listeners, the better your message sounds to them. Clients need something from you: your knowledge, products, or services. They're not seeing you because they're lonely.

A few months back, after meeting with a client on Wall Street, I learned from my administrative assistant that an executive from a famous international luxury clothes retailer wanted me to stop by as soon as possible *that morning* to present an outline of my services. I said I'd be there in 20 minutes and had the cabdriver head to Madison Avenue.

In the taxi on the way to the retailer I jotted down eight essential questions I knew I needed to ask before I could begin selling my services. When I arrived, the head of operations greeted me with a welcoming smile and said, "Hi, I'm Beverly. I manage sales and operations training. What do you have for me today?"

I was taken aback. In 22 years of selling, I'd never been asked this question. I felt like a waiter and was tempted to reply, "Well, I have some roast chicken today and some tuna. But the tuna's not so fresh. Maybe you'd like the pasta?"

My potential client was asking for my seminar presentation immediately after our introduction, something that normally takes me weeks to prepare. She wanted me to jump right in instead of letting me interview her to uncover her specific training needs and assess the strengths and weaknesses of the company's salespeople.

This happens frequently to all of us. People want information and they want it now. And you're tempted to jump back with an easy answer (because, after all, you probably have a good idea of what to say). But don't. The underlying foundation of a successful sale is to understand the client's unique needs before you try to make a sale.

When I was growing up, I used to make hospital rounds with my father, a New York surgeon. Rounds would take all morning. I'll never forget my dad hovering over a patient and sweetly, with empathy, asking a series of fact-finding questions to discern progress from the day before. Patients would brighten up immediately upon seeing him and answer him thoughtfully and honestly. He was so concentrated on the responses that when I would ask him when we were going to lunch he wouldn't even hear me. When he was with a patient, a marching band could have trooped down the hall and he wouldn't have heard it.

This is the sort of interaction that needs to occur whenever you meet with a client. It begins with preparation, your efforts to create the link between "doctor" and "patient." Each of us has an obligation to thoroughly understand and know whom we're speaking with before we embark on our message to them.

Let's get back to the luxury retailer. After Beverly asked what I had for her, I responded by giving her an agenda of how I thought our time should be spent. "I thought about our meeting on the way here in the taxi," I said, "and I realized that there is so much that I could say about my services that the most efficient way for us to meet today would be for me to ask you a series of questions to determine your specific training needs and then for us to look at what I have to offer and see if there is a match."

With this comment she let out a laugh and then replied, "You just got yourself an hour." She explained, "I've said no to

4

three other consultants because they never asked me any questions about my organization when I first met with them. They jumped right in and took off with it."

I was pleased with the opportunity that had been given to me, but also stunned that so many of my professional colleagues made this simple error. I've come to learn over the years that many people on sales calls miss out on this cornerstone of success.

People want solutions to their needs, but they won't allow someone the chance to lead them if they feel that the leader is on automatic and only concerned with his or her own self.

My father has always said, "No two patients are the same. If you decide to treat one patient the same as the other, you put at least one of them at risk."

In my career, you honor others by treating them like no other individual you've ever dealt with before. This is how you stay fresh, on target, and successful. It's also one of the best ways to kick Murphy out the door.

MAKING REAL ADVANCES IN SALES SKILLS

Think about an upcoming sales call. Your first obligation is to gather a fair amount of information about your client and your client's business. Write down five questions you need answered. Reread the questions several times. You'll notice that these five questions directly lead to five more questions that need answering too. The ability to develop a growing list of questions—

things you need to know in order to best serve the client—indicates you are already making progress in your sales skills.

This type of skill building is an example of the simple, but vital lessons I impart to my clients who seek to make real advances in their sales abilities. This is also the core of this book—easy-to-follow lessons that keep you in charge and keep Murphy at bay.

Of course, Murphy is a wily deal killer—and a pain in the neck. He likes to sneak in when you least expect it, come a-callin' without an invitation, make himself at home, and track mud through the house when he does. And you know what: That's okay! Part of what you'll learn here is that Murphy never goes away totally, but you can totally handle it.

And that's just the beginning. This book aims to make you the best in the business. From the moment you start to research your client to the follow-up you'll make after a successful sale, this book will make a positive difference for you and for those you serve.

It will also make a difference in our profession. One of my overarching goals is to help bring respect back to sales. I consider it my responsibility, and I want you to consider it your responsibility too.

It's not a matter of wishing. It's understanding technique, utilizing skills, avoiding unnecessary mistakes, having a sincere desire to help the client, and spending lots and lots of time preparing. This book will guide you through all these things to put you at the top and show Murphy the door.

I know it can happen. I've seen it tens of thousands of times.

1

ANATOMY OF A
SALES CALL

A few years back I was called in to advise an advertising sales-woman from a luxury magazine. I was to accompany her on sales calls, acting as a "consultant to the magazine's Web site," to listen to how the magazine was articulated to help me add to the site. Before our first sales call together, she briefed me on the next client, a retailer of expensive bracelets.

Within moments after we walked into the office, the client tossed a copy of The Robb Report *in front of her and challenged, "What can you give me that they can't?"*

Instantly thrown off guard, she spent the rest of her one-shot appointment defending her magazine against the competition. Unfortunately, no matter how good her presentation or arguments were, she was lost, because he set the stage and was now running the show, lobbing one rapid-fire question after another.

The saleswoman went in thinking only of making a sale—she wanted another notch on her rifle without regard for the customer's best interests. Instead of another notch, though, she ended up staring down Murphy's barrel.

What should she have done? After the magazine landed in front of her, she should have looked at her customer and said, "You obviously like The Robb Report *a lot. Why? How does it serve your needs? How does it fit into what you want for your company?"*

The lesson is that you need to have a course of action for a sales call and be ready to set that course of action. It begins with understanding the anatomy of a sales call. That understanding leads to confidence, which translates to control. That way, when someone throws you a whammy, you can turn it to your advantage (think judo) and get back on your own track, in control and on the way to achieving your agenda.

Fifteen years ago the president of American Express TRS, Thomas Ryder, now chief executive officer (CEO) of *Reader's Digest*, gave me a marching order that I have never forgotten. After interviewing him at length regarding the sales force that I was going to begin coaching and developing, he said, "I am hiring you to bring respect back to the salespeople of this company."

I have never forgotten this marching order and have chosen it as my career mission. This chapter outlines a simple, yet highly professional way to communicate and sell an idea to anyone, anywhere, and gain the respect of that individual, just as Mr. Ryder knew was right.

You're probably thinking that you're not reading this book to hear a story about respect, but to find out how to make a sale. Okay, here it is, plain and simple: The main reason a sale isn't made is because the sale wasn't planned. So how does that relate to respect?

In order to make a sale, both parties must agree that the product or service being sold solves a problem or fills a gap, a problem or gap that both you and your client mutually agree upon. This goes right back to respect. The reason why salespeople aren't given the respect they want is usually because they've neglected to engage in the *process* that will give them and their recommendations the respect needed to consummate the sale.

At the heart of the process is understanding that you really don't sell anything to anyone. Instead, what you do is let people self-realize the benefit of your product or service. Clients will naturally choose things that they can see will benefit them and their circumstances.

This process shows respect for the client, and it shows you that when fully informed the client will make the right decision. This is why the most effective journalists need never divulge their personal opinions on any matter. In all likelihood they do have an opinion, for example, on the politicians they cover. But if they are confident that their writings are based on the facts, they will trust that their readers can come to their own best judgments when presented with the facts. Give your clients the essential information they need. Trust them to make the right decision.

Respect for the client, in turn, brings respect to sales and to you. This book is dedicated to keeping respect front and center.

I intend to make you aware of all the Murphy's laws that accompany a sale, from your initial thought of whom to sell to and what to sell them to the actual handshake consummating the transaction. When you know the pitfalls, you can avoid them and not worry about mistakes; instead, you can concentrate on the sale.

UNDERSTANDING THE ANATOMY

The first step to understanding sales is to understand the anatomy of a sales call. My father, a surgeon, always said, "unless you completely understand the anatomy of the human body you cannot perform a mistake-free operation." When I was growing up, I used to see my father at our kitchen table studying his anatomy books at six in the morning as I was getting ready for school. By that time, he would have already been at it for a couple of hours, preparing for his morning operations.

Sometimes he'd outline the planned operations for me (in much too graphic detail for 6 a.m.) and explain the exact series of cuts and ligations he was planning.

He'd also explain every possible problem, i.e., Murphy's law, that could possibly arise and sabotage the planned operation. By the time he was done it was clear that this list of problems was longer and clearly of more concern than the actual operation he was performing.

The link between my dad's work and ours as salespeople is quite similar. The *major* question to ask yourself is, "Am I doing my client homework and studying for this sale as diligently as any good doctor so that I can stay in control of the sale and deftly handle the objections and questions that will surely come my way throughout the selling process?"

Occasionally I would talk with my dad about handling emergencies in the operating room. He once explained to me how certain doctors remained cool under pressure and how others panicked. It was fascinating to listen to him detail an operation to the point where Murphy's law actually showed up and then hear what he or another surgeon actually did to overcome the problem and keep control over the outcome of the operation.

I remember one story of a surgeon who just lost it. He started to choke under the pressure of several unplanned events that completely altered the operation flow and forced him to lateral the case to his attending physician. I asked my father, "What happened, Dad? How could this guy do that?" He told me how the surgeon had not foreseen the ramifications of the cuts that he made and did not remember the surrounding veins that his cuts severed simultaneously. I know this is a bit messy for a sales book, but this story serves as a perfect metaphor for a planning process that accounts for anything that in any way ruins the "operation" (your presentation). When my father recounted that story to me, I understood the reason for his early morning study.

SIX MAIN PHASES OF A CLIENT MEETING

MURPHY STRIKES

I know I'm supposed to keep my greeting tight and bright, but last week I began by asking a client, "How are you?" which I figured was a safe enough opening. But, as Ann Landers once put it, I asked for a happy note and got an organ recital. My client immediately went into a sad-sack story of how "things are in the toilet, my boss is on me like crazy, I got new product I can't move," and on and on. It was almost depressing and really put a crimp in my enthusiasm. How could I acknowledge his problems and stay upbeat?

Client meetings consist of six main phases:

1. Opening comments
2. Stating the meeting agenda
3. Probing and listening
4. Presentation
5. Resolving questions and objections
6. Closing

I know you're thinking that if this is so simple, what's the problem? Look closely: Murphy is all over this agenda. At the point of the handshake, even before the opening comments, a client could say, "Hey, I've been meeting with representatives from your competitor. Here's their rate. Can you beat it? If not, then my business goes to them."

Not a pretty picture to have right after you've shaken hands, but it does happen. Consider the client who answers his phone during meetings or the one who always interrupts. You can stay in control of the meeting and solve all those frustrations if you make your intentions known at the start of the meeting.

You must provide clients with an agenda for the meeting to prevent them or anything else from derailing you. This is not to say you will never get derailed. You will. But, you need to understand how to control the conversation in the face of these derailments and gracefully return your clients to your original agenda. Of course, this is easier said than done!

It's important to examine each of these phases of the anatomy of a sales call. I'll also discuss some Murphy's laws that come with each phase.

PHASE 1—OPENING COMMENTS

The opening of a meeting is when you're most vulnerable and Murphy is most liable to show up. If you're not prepared with opening comments, then the pressure of meeting new clients combined with other pressures can lead to an instant derailment opportunity the moment you arrive.

Here's why: All clients you will ever see have many, many other things on their minds besides the ones you want to help them with. All these demands follow clients throughout their day, just like the obligations you have with your own job. But, you've got to deal with yours and they have to deal with theirs. During a meeting, however, you've got to deal with your own pressures and, for the purposes of your presentation, your clients' pressures too.

Empathize with their burdens and never discount them as being less important than what you'll be discussing at the sales meeting. Be sure to remain flexible enough to have a few moments to discuss these tangential pressures at an appropriate time in the meeting.

One quick aside: Empathy is critical here. It is very different than sympathy, which is the sameness of feeling, a feeling of approval of or agreement with an idea, cause, etc. Empathy is the projection of one's own personality into the personality of another in order to understand the other person better, the ability to share in another's emotions, thoughts, or feelings. The reason why it's important to distinguish between these emotions is because too often we get seduced into being sympathetic to our client's situation and pressures versus being empathetic to them.

Sympathy offers a shoulder to cry on. Empathy looks for a solution.

Later in this book we will cover the importance of research and probing, in part because it allows you to discover preemptively the pressures and problems that you will be walking into when you meet with your client. The master salesperson determines which pressures and problems are legitimate stops to a client accepting a recommendation and which ones are not. Only empathy can show you the difference.

PHASE 2—STATING THE MEETING AGENDA

Establishing an agenda for your sales calls gives you control over them, despite the pressures and headaches that your clients are feeling the moment they meet you. One of my clients, Jim Berrien, the president of Forbes, has long maintained that "in selling it's always good to be paranoid."

In other words, always prepare for the worst-case scenario based on your research. Prepare specific responses to these potential pressures and problems that can and will surface during a presentation. By constructing specific responses ahead of time you can maintain control of your sales call, even when a client throws a major objection at you right after you've said hello.

It starts by stating the agenda clearly and at the very beginning. Here's an example:

John, I was thinking about our time today, and I realized from my research on your company that there are several questions I need to ask you in order to properly present the linkage between it and my organization. I'd like to ask you these questions first, draw the connection, and then finish up with any questions you and I may have from our discussion. It's now 11:15 a.m. I'd say we'll be completed by noon. Is that okay?

Try it. It's amazing how much control you will gain by this respectful opening. Clients like this approach because it tells them that the salesperson is prepared, confident, and knowledgeable about the proper techniques to use to handle a sales call. This agenda also communicates that while the beginning of the call is not the ideal time to address the client's pressures and problems, there will be more than enough opportunities to do so during the meeting.

PHASE 3—PROBING AND LISTENING

You've presented your agenda to the client, you got an okay to go ahead, and now it's time to begin the most important part of the sales call: probing and listening. Your prior research hasn't been so much about discovering information as it has been about discovering information you need, but don't have. It leads you to this moment, when you will ask the critical questions that will pinpoint how and why you fit in with your client. You will *probe* with the right questions and you will *listen* carefully to the responses.

In Chapter 7, I'll go into the questioning and listening process in depth, but, in brief, this is the phase of the sales call where you verify your desk research and establish the problem and opportunity relationship that makes clear to your client the importance of accepting your product or service.

Your research will have already dictated the form of your questions, questions that you've written down ahead of time. These questions should communicate your knowledge of your clients' businesses, the products they sell, their competitive set (who they're up against), the marketplace challenges they face, and their overall track record.

The ease or difficulty of finding this information varies widely. For instance, there are times when data cannot be found for privately held companies. Chapter 2 covers a wide range of reconnaissance techniques tailored to help you gather your research. Research allows you to craft appropriate, professional questions. You'll learn the importance of making questions seamless, constructing a rhythm so that questions flow naturally one to the next.

But, what about Murphy? What happens when you're thrown off track by a tangential thought by your client? This is why it's important to always have your questions written out before your sales call. Now, after you acknowledge and discuss the tangential issue ("Yeah, those Mets really are amazing!"), you have a place to return to in order to get back to business. In my field research I have witnessed too many cases where a salesperson never recovered from these types of tangents. Folks who get tangled in tangents end up losing control of their sales calls—time runs out and clients' interests shift away from you to themselves.

PHASE 4—PRESENTATION

Ah, the time has finally come for you to sing, to deliver the goods. First thing to remember: Don't sing too long. Next thing to remember: Sing on key or the audition is over (and you won't be invited back anytime soon).

This part of the sales call is the time when you present your recommendation in the most genuine, caring way possible. It is the time to make the match that you hinted at in the beginning of the meeting when you stated your agenda. It is the time for advocacy.

A dear friend, the head of a law firm, recently asked me to help him design a course for his attorneys. They were not selling anything, per se, but they are advocates and that's the subject of the course. Advocacy means to speak or write in support of or, in other words, promote and back something or someone because you're a true believer. My friend had observed that his attorneys needed sharper advocacy skills. Upon closer examination, we discovered that they specifically needed to strengthen how they organize their content and how they physically deliver their comments.

As a lawyer, my friend understands the importance of advocacy. He realizes that his attorneys only get one shot at a clear, concise statement of advocacy to juries. You, too, must have a very clear, simple, distilled presentation that advocates what you have to offer in a way that lets clients understand and accept your recommendations.

PHASE 5—RESOLVING QUESTIONS AND OBJECTIONS

Here is a favorite Murphy hangout: the question and answer part of the sales call, a make-or-break moment. In Chapter 9, I discuss the many ways Murphy likes to infiltrate the situation and how you can cut him off at the pass.

Suffice it to say here that your preparation and reconnaissance are paramount to your ability to resolve your client's questions and concerns and remain in control of the sales call. It's not hard to imagine a client asking a series of difficult questions, not being satisfied with your answers, and then concluding that she'll wait 6 months before deciding. All your hard work has then been put on perpetual hold because you couldn't handle the tough questions.

Can you be 100 percent bulletproof? No, but you can be 100 percent prepared to the best of your knowledge. You can look behind each question, determine its source and relative importance, and then do your best to properly resolve it in the context of the need for your product or service—a need you've already established by mutual agreement.

Questions can arise at any stage of the selling process. But, no matter when they occur, remain calm. Instead of worrying, pinpoint the specific question being posed. Determine if you have sufficient information to answer the question at that time. If so, answer it. If not, then write it down in your portfolio, and offer a time in the next 24 to 48 hours when you will call back with the correct answer.

PHASE 6—CLOSING

Closing is not always about "signing on the line which is dotted," as yelled by Alec Baldwin in *GlenGarry GlenRoss*. Closing is about determining the next logical step in the advocacy process. It is about understanding what needs to occur next in order to serve your client in the most professional way. It is about being the first one to articulate the next step from your meeting.

This is not to say that your client should not be the one to determine the next step. But, generally, it is your responsibility to present clients with your understanding of what should happen next. If you're way off base, the client will tell you, I promise. But, even if you're wrong, you still will at least have discovered what they don't want to do, which is halfway to knowing what they do want to do.

If nothing else, this tells you whether or not your clients have followed your presentation to its logical next step. If not, you first need to assess your handling of the sales call and if you presented each phase of the sales call correctly.

You are also now in a position to look behind their idea of the next step by asking several questions. Chapter 10 covers in depth how to close a sales call and what specifically to look and listen for during the sales call to determine the correct next step, the one that's unlikely to be contested.

STEVE BUSTS MURPHY

You start off with what you think is the safest opening possible—"How are you?"—and you get a violin solo. Don't fret. First, take a step back and assess why your client came at you that way. It's probably one of two things. First, he does this to everyone and at least you know going forward that you've got a crying towel on your hands and can plan accordingly for your next meeting with him.

The second possibility is that he actually trusts you and is comfortable enough with you to let his guard down and let it all hang out, regardless of your comfort level. Take it as a compliment to you and the type of relationship you have with him.

Still, you're eager to put the meeting on a more positive note. Comment about your own trials and tribulations from a confident perspective.

> Boy, I know what you mean about all of this being frustrating. Currently there are several issues I'm juggling with that demand a huge amount of time to do them right. I guess though, given what's gone on in the world, we're pretty lucky that we get to deal with these issues instead of what some other people are dealing with. Hopefully our discussion today will be the bright spot in today for you and me.

See if he doesn't lighten up and then present your agenda for the meeting.

BOTTOM LINE

Expect any possibility when you go into a meeting, but remain confident that you can set the tone just as well as set the agenda. Offer a considerate ear, but keep the meeting moving forward and up.

CHAPTER

2

THE BEST WAY
TO BEAT MURPHY

RECONNAISSANCE RULES

---

*It's one of my favorite roles, hired to tag along as an "assistant"
to watch a salesperson on a sales call, in this case a visit to the
CEO of a major supermarket chain in the Chicago area. I was
there as an observer to see if I could understand why the CEO
had been resistant to the salesperson on earlier calls.*

*It's part of my work. People pay me to watch a salesperson.
But, sometimes, I'd do it for free because the information it
reveals is so staggering.*

*I sat watching as the salesperson talked about his com-
pany, the greatness of his product, the great new promotion
his company was offering. What he said was accurate, but it
had nothing to do with the concerns of his client.*

It's normal procedure for me to observe the salesperson and make my analysis later. But this was an exception. I watched quietly until I realized the sale was about to go down the tubes. I had to step in. With a brief probing, I began to uncover some basics.

I asked the executive how long he'd been in the supermarket business. His whole professional life, he said, and he was, in fact, the owner of the chain. From there, I asked what sort of changes he was hoping to bring to his stores. He explained that he was frustrated that the higher-margin items, such as catering and bakery goods, were not moving as well as he wanted. I asked who his current customers were, and he told me they were stay-at-home types, "cocooning" was the phrase he used, who didn't rely on the higher-margin items. I then asked who the supermarket considered the ideal customer base and which large-margin items it had targeted for greater sales and found that the CEO wanted more upscale customers who spent more, more frequently. I then showed how the service the salesperson and I were offering responded precisely to the CEO's needs.

Murphy is a guy who doesn't listen. He only talks.

If these questions had been written out beforehand, they would have been asked at the start of the meeting.

It's not easy to do everything that's required to do a good job in sales. But, it's a lot easier than not doing what's required.

Prepared questions let you understand the customer's needs. By pinpointing the need, you create a link between your product and your client—the single most important basis for a sale. The only way to do that right is if you have done the research to know what to ask.

The phrase "reconnaissance rules" is a double entendre. First, reconnaissance rules are a set of 10 rules that if followed will make sure you've done your homework in preparation for your meeting. Second, reconnaissance rules means that reconnaissance, as a research methodology, is the single most significant facet for a successful sales call. It rules.

Someone once said, the will to win is meaningless without the will to prepare. In war, reconnaissance is discovering enemy positions and arms. It's a survey, an examination of the enemy. It works the same way in a sales call: Get the lay of the land ahead of time and use that information to your advantage. A keen offense depends on knowing everything possible about the other side, and successful presentations require knowing each audience—from Wall Street barons to a Girl Scout troop. It begins with understanding them and knowing what they need and want.

Reconnaissance is not just a convenience, it's a requirement. You are not going on a sales call because you're lonely. Customers don't see you because they need more friends. You are there to fill a need. Otherwise, why bother?

Through reconnaissance, you come to the sales call ready to explain the aspects of your company that a client wants to know. If you know that a quick turnaround on deliveries is important to your client, for example, you'll be prepared to share information about how you can ensure quick deliveries, present case histories of your company's on-time record, and explain how deliveries are guaranteed to arrive on time. If exclusivity is an objective, you'll know how your products or services will bring that desired cache to the company.

THE 10 RULES OF RECONNAISSANCE

MURPHY STRIKES

My new client was a huge corporation, with global reach and many, many lines. My problem wasn't getting enough data, it was having too much. I felt overwhelmed by the amount of information I had to slog through. How could I have narrowed it down to suit my purposes?

A successful sales call, one where Murphy is clearly not invited to sit in, is based on preparation. PREPARE. PREPARE. PREPARE. And there's only one way to start: You need to conduct the best roundup of information possible. You must pull out all the stops to get every bit you can find, anywhere you can find it.

In order to have a Murphy-free meeting, you need to prepare each time, every time. No two clients will ever be the same, just as no two salespeople are the same. Yet, I'm amazed at how many salespeople are on autopilot when they go on a sales call. They arrive with just their own company's data, media kit, or sales presentation. What doesn't come with them is a series of questions crafted from good client reconnaissance.

Selling by nature is a repetitive act, and it is easy to lose your creativity with repetition. But, if you lose your creativity, you lose your empathy toward your client and you give control to Murphy. To avoid going into autopilot, perform specific research that will reveal clients for the unique creatures they are. Every client, when studied closely, has a one-of-a-kind profile, a place in the world like no one else. We live in a jaded era, and it's easy to become weary. Don't fall into this trap.

Your responsibility in the world of sales is to first respect clients by understanding and accepting their uniqueness and to then demonstrate that respect through your knowledge of who they are as evidenced by the recommendations you will provide.

A solid client reconnaissance plan provides you with the information needed to craft unique and sophisticated questions for your client meeting. Your research gives you a three-dimensional view of your client. Good research will lead you to want to ask certain specific questions not only to verify that research, but also to understand where your client is headed and how your client plans on getting there. How can you recommend your product or service without understanding where it fits into your client's overall business strategy? Salespeople who sell without this linkage risk selling bad business. They risk hurting their own reputation and the reputation of their company.

Due diligence will take you below the waterline of the proverbial iceberg. By seeing the iceberg almost in its entirety (you need a probing meeting to fully reveal the entire iceberg, as you will discover later in this book), you can craft questions that convince your client that you have done your homework and have earned the right to ask these sophisticated questions.

Showcasing your research through tailored, probing questions communicates much more than just your knowledge. It communicates concern and respect for the company you are meeting with. This illustration of respect will in turn earn you respect during your first meeting. Once you've earned that respect, you'll likely be rewarded with honest responses to your questions. These honest responses complete your reconnaissance and allow you to craft a tailored presentation that genuinely solves a problem.

Follow these rules to cover what you need to know.

The 10 Rules of Reconnaissance

1. Know your company's history with the client.

2. Know the client's marketing goals.

3. Know the sales trends of the client's business.

4. Know the client's market share.

5. Know the client's competitive position.

6. Know the pricing of the client's products.

7. Know the client's distribution network.

8. Know the client's target audience.

9. Know the key contacts in the client's company.

10. Know everything you can possibly learn from every available legal source.

These basic rules will serve as a template to get the core information you need to understand your client. Once you've acquired this knowledge, you're ready to prepare a list of questions that will begin your interview process at your meeting.

STEVE BUSTS MURPHY

The typical problem when you conduct reconnaissance is getting enough information. But, when you work with an enormous company, the difficulty isn't getting enough information, it's getting enough of the right information.

First, understand the specific scope of the client you will be dealing with. She works in a specific division, so find articles related to that division. Salomon Smith Barney is a huge company owned by Citigroup, an even bigger company. If you are going to see someone in public finance at Salomon Smith Barney, you need to find out about public finance and not waste your time researching the private side. American Express has many divisions. When I go to see someone in travel-related services, I go to that data—not the corporate card and not consultants, none of that applies.

In large companies, you need to understand the direction of your client. Follow that line: What areas are the responsibility of your direct contact? Where is his part of the business now? What's going on with the business health of that segment?

BOTTOM LINE

In large companies, narrow your reconnaissance focus to the segment of the industry represented by your direct contact.

TURNING OVER EVERY ROCK

MURPHY STRIKES

A friend who used to work for my prospective client knew I was preparing for a big meeting with the client and gave me some proprietary information about the company that would have gotten him fired had he still worked there. It was helpful, but it felt wrong. What limits was I responsible for placing on myself in my research?

INFORMATION-GATHERING SOURCES

Effective reconnaissance means going on a scavenger hunt as you track down your information. You become a detective, sleuthing in odd corners as well as along well-worn paths for your information. By collecting your data from a wide variety of sources you have the opportunity to uncover key facts that will serve you in your sales calls.

Information-gathering sources can be categorized into three main areas: internal sources, customer sources, and external sources.

Internal sources

Know thyself. Know how your company operates, how it relates to your client in particular, and how it relates to the world, in general. Know the good and the bad. If your company sponsors a 10K run to raise money for cancer research, you should know that. If it helped create a SuperFund site, you should know that too.

Your company may have a history with your client. Know everything about that history. Are your products or services in use now? How big is the account? What did it look like a year ago? What will that account look like a year from now? Have previous products or services your company offered failed with the client? Which ones have been successes? Find out why. Talk to colleagues. Look at your files.

Have others in your company tried to make a sale, but failed? What was the problem? Determine where the failure occurred. Was the fit wrong? Did personalities make the difference?

Will this be your company's first attempt at business with the client? If so, examine your company product and service profile to determine what parts will be right for the new client. If you had to decide on just one product for the new client, which one would it be? Why?

Finally, your client may ask you some basic questions about your company. Know the basics, including:

- Stock price

- Personnel changes

- Earnings worldwide

- Plans for international business

- Markets targeted for growth

- Strategic direction

- Product changes, including new and discontinued items

Customer sources

Your client's company probably has a vast body of publicly available information. Look at it all. Look through the self-promotional language to get to the nitty-gritty (year-end budgetary adjustments mentioned in the annual report, for example, usually mean the company didn't make a profit). Include the following in your customer sources:

- Annual reports

- Company newsletters

- Corporate statements

- In-house publications, such as staff newspapers

- Conversations with present and former employees

- Company Web site

External sources

They say we live in the information age and it's true. There is endless information available on almost every subject. Your client is no exception. Most data sources are far from exotic and are easily available. What you need to know can come from some fairly obvious sources, but don't overlook them just because they're obvious.

Interested in how many outlets of the retailer are in your area? Look in the phone book. Want to know who services a supermarket's racks? Go the store and see which trucks pull up during the average business day.

As you go about your research, be sure to include the following sources:

- Newspapers, business publications

- Industry reports

- Professional associations, guilds, and boards

- Association reports

- Market research and information from clients' competitors

- Industry conferences

Tap all three source areas to the fullest extent possible. Keep detailed notes of what you discover, confirming information when necessary and eliminating false leads.

STEVE BUSTS MURPHY

Your research represents honest due diligence. I repeat, *honest due diligence.* Ethics require that you neither steal information nor lie to get it. It's the same for information that otherwise you would not legally have access to. In this case, the information came into your hands without any untoward action on your part. It's now part of your body of knowledge for better or worse.

How you use that knowledge, however, is where you may get botched up. If there is even the slightest chance that your client smells any impropriety on your part, deep-six the data; it's not worth keeping it. Your client may well know that you work with a former employee and may be ready to pounce if you bring up information that you would not otherwise know.

Further, if word gets around that you use questionable information derived from inappropriate sources, you'll only add baggage to your reputation and who needs that?

BOTTOM LINE

Knowledge is important. What you do with the knowledge is more important.

CHANCE FAVORS THE PREPARED MIND

MURPHY STRIKES

Others in my company had tried to wrangle my target client before me, so when I tried to get them to help me out in my research—information on things they had already uncovered—they stonewalled, as if to say, "If I can't have that client, I'm sure not going to help you get the client." I know they have valuable information, but I also understand their reluctance to just give it up to the next person down the line. How do I finesse this?

Every client is a puzzle. You have to figure out that puzzle. Discovering the solution begins with your reconnaissance. When it was time for me to meet with executives of a major New York bank, I first had to know the banking industry. My clients deserved a salesperson who did everything possible to become knowledgeable about their organization.

Your reconnaissance should answer fundamental questions that reveal the specifics of the client. So as you do research, write down questions. If you discover the answers during your research ("Who are the top five players in the industry?"), then refine the question ("Who among the top five players has seen the most growth in the past decade? Why?")

For my meeting with the bank, I first went to the American Banking Association Web site. It was a great start. The information, however, was global. My next step was to go to the company Web site. There I looked for

- Products sold
- Company history
- Sales volume
- Corporate direction
- Association membership
- Company challenges

- E-business strategy

- Locations

Importantly, I also went to many of the bank's competitors' Web sites to better understand how my client stood among the competition.

I then used a template of research points that I perform for each of my clients. I went from global to local resources, and my questions helped me create a profile of the client, as a way to understand the client's uniqueness.

The value of the template is that it simplifies the reconnaissance actions you need to take each time you meet with a client. With a solid reconnaissance template, all you have to do is fill it out! (You may wonder, "How unique is this approach if it uses a template?" The answer is that uniqueness isn't revealed in how you do your research. It's in what that research reveals and then what you do with it.)

By developing habits of good reconnaissance, you then spend your time digesting what your research has brought you and, from there, determining what sets your client apart. Murphy slimes things up when you think that one client's issues are the same or similar to another client's. First, we run the risk of arrogance through this inappropriate homogenization. Homogenization is for milk, not clients. Second, we risk appearing unsophisticated through our lack of understanding of our client's world. Two strikes and you're almost out! And for what? There is no justification for being unsophisticated in today's business world, especially with so much data at our fingertips, from newspapers to online sources.

Here are some of the things I needed to find out about my banking client; these questions apply to almost every client you will have:

- Where does the organization stand in the market?

- What has the CEO declared as goals?

- What products does the organization sell?

- What's the competition?

- What's the organization's structure?

- Who are the decision makers?

- What's the political climate?

- What's the client's prior history with my company?

- What's it like inside a branch of the bank? How is it run?

- What's the growth strategy?

- Who is the target customer?

- What are the organization's latest promotions?

- What has the media said about the client?

Almost all this basic information is available to the public. Use the Internet, library, or other easy-access sources to obtain it.

STEVE BUSTS MURPHY

The one place you expect you won't have difficulty finding information is from your colleagues. What reasonable person wouldn't want to help a colleague help the company they both work for? But, there are a lot of unreasonable people out there. If you're getting the brush-off from a fellow worker, chalk it up to a matter of (misplaced) pride. Forget him. When you're refused help, simply say "no problem" with a smile and move on to sources that will help you. Each day that goes by, the colleague will just feel worse for stiffing you, knowing that a colleague was left high and dry by one of his own. By the way, you didn't ask, but let me advise: Keep your eye on this one. It could be trouble.

BOTTOM LINE

To paraphrase an old saying, when a door is closed, a window is opened. If you get rebuffed at one stage in your reconnaissance, move on to the next.

GOING FROM MACRO TO MICRO IN 20 QUESTIONS

MURPHY STRIKES

I write out my questions ahead of time, but inevitably the answers I receive lead to areas that totally surprise me. Even simple questions, such as, "What goals have you set for the coming season?" are met with answers such as, "Goals consistent with our company's objectives since its founding." When my questions get a whack answer, how do I respond?

Develop a minimum of 20 questions prior to any interview. This is an organic process, that is, where one question naturally leads to the next. Here's an example of how you might prioritize your questions:

1. How do you grow your business?

2. What are your plans to grow the business in the coming year?

3. What are your current challenges?

4. Describe your customer profile.

5. Who is your most profitable customer?

6. What new customers would you like to target?

7. How do you think your business will look 5 years from now?

8. What are the company's annual gross sales (prior research may answer this)?

9. How was the volume last month?

10. What was the average ticket?

11. What are your expected returns from recent investments?

12. Has your company made significant recent overall strategy changes?

13. Are there any shifts in short- or long-term marketing strategies?

14. How has that affected your work here?

15. Have you taken on any marketing partners?

16. What's your objective in doing that?

17. Are there any new advertising campaigns planned?

18. What other vehicles are you using for customer outreach?

19. How much time are you going to give yourself to reach your goals?

20. How do you, the salesperson, fit in with reaching those goals?

These are general questions, but they give you a good example of how questions naturally lead one to the next. Writing your questions out ahead of time is a critical component of your reconnaissance.

Each client is different, of course, so your list of questions will be different for each, too. A magazine advertising salesperson who I helped prepare to meet with a maker of nutrition bars, knew he needed to craft 20 open-ended questions that would allow him to narrow down the company's needs and determine how what he had to offer might fit in with those needs. The questions we developed were the following:

1. Your target market is 18- to 24-year-olds. Describe who a typical person from this age group is. Will the description of this typical person be the same 5 years from now?

2. How do you intend to expand your market?

3. Which markets represent the strongest growth?

4. Who is your biggest retailer?

5. Is there any seasonality to your product?

6. Your main competitor has 10 new flavors. What brand extensions are you planning?

7. How is your product different from that of the competition?

8. Is Brand A in your competitive set? Who else do you consider in that set?

9. Besides offering a similar product, why are they competitors? (Do they have a similar target audience, regional presence, or advertising thrust?)

10. How do you select your advertising media?

11. What sponsorships are you involved in?

12. Describe promotional programs aimed at increasing sales.

13. Your ad campaigns recently expanded to television. Do you intend to use integrated ad programs for next year or do these campaigns reach different audiences?

14. If your goals are reached, what do you foresee as your advertising program further down the road?

15. Describe your creative thrust for next year.

16. Last year, you spent about $3 million. Is that amount going to increase for this year?

17. Last year, you advertised in (major sports) magazine. What was the rationale there?

18. What funds remain for advertising this year?

19. What's your perception of my magazine?

20. What do you want to make happen this year that I should know about?

STEVE BUSTS MURPHY

When in doubt about a client's response—let's say that what they answered really threw you—ask another question. There are many benefits of asking another question. You are seen as being concerned and thoughtful. The other benefit to asking a follow-up question is getting a reading on the level of participation and partnership from your client. It's possible that you've got a wise guy who is playing hard to get until you reestablish your purpose and credibility. Or, you may have someone who has been burned before who is skeptical of everyone. You don't know at this point, and you need to figure it out to determine how to successfully communicate with this person.

BOTTOM LINE

Questions are for discovering information. Be ready to accept the information you asked for, regardless of whether or not it's what you expected.

3

LOOK OUT FOR MURPHY
MY FAILURE AND WELCOME TO IT

At the beginning of a major executive's retirement dinner, the guest of honor confided in me that he was extremely anxious and nervous about the speech he would have to give after listening to all the expected accolades. It's easy to see why a situation like that can put a person on edge. I know people who blush at a mere compliment—imagine a 30-minute barrage of it.

But, blushing would not do. Here was a guy who had spent his career leading a huge corporation and he was expected to go out with that sense of leadership intact. This was not the time for an "ah-shucks" response.

During the main course and in the minutes leading up to his speech, I explained to the executive that the speech he was about to give wasn't really about him. It was about acknowledging his direct reports and peers for the great moments and lessons about life that he was able to experience and share with them during his time at the company.

Murphy loves a case of the nerves: Whatever makes you nervous he will surely try to make the center of your attention. If you are nervous about the focus being on you, then move it off of you and focus it where it will make a difference and, in turn, keep you in control.

When it came time for my friend to give his thanks, I was blown away by how well he understood and used the coaching to his advantage. The speech was great.

If Murphy ever lived anywhere, it's in the house of self-doubt. Just like my client at his retirement, it's only natural to have second thoughts about a key presentation, especially a major sales presentation or speech. To begin to "ghostbust" Murphy, understand and accept this fact of life. Listen folks, until we turn into rosebushes it will only be natural to get spooked sometime.

Many great Broadway actors, no matter how many years they've had on stage, still get butterflies before a big performance. They're anxious and excited, but they use this energy to steel themselves, to commit themselves to giving their all to their role and to their audience. It's not for nothing that they're called professionals.

But, remember: Murphy comes in only because you let him in. The essence of this chapter and the essence of this book is to teach you to stay confident and in control. Now, you may be saying to yourself, "Great! Just what I need, a wiseacre author shortcutting the chapter on what I'm most interested in by minimizing the issue." Relax. No shortcuts here. This entire chapter—and book—is about kicking Murphy's butt. But we're going to do it one step at a time.

First, take this simple oath: I solemnly swear to accept that it is only human to worry that Murphy will screw up my sales call. I pledge to put Murphy into proper perspective and place myself above him and in control of him based upon my solid confidence in myself and the preparation of my message.

What I say is simple; the way you do it, not so. Let's get started by examining the preparation of your message and presentation, and then we'll look at its delivery and how to keep a clear head in the process.

EIGHT ESSENTIALS TO PREPARING YOUR MESSAGE AND PRESENTATION

MURPHY STRIKES

Sometimes as I prepare for a meeting, I get preoccupied with too many scenarios—What if they want to know if I'm up on last year's sales? What if they're interested in a multiyear pricing schedule? What if they ask me about my hometown team? (This comes up so many times and I hate sports!) I get so tied up trying to prepare for all the possible questions, I can barely keep it all straight. How can I be ready and not overwhelmed?

There are eight rules that, when followed properly, will help you master your meeting preparation:

1. Work alone.

2. Practice makes a master.

3. Know the objections you'll get.

4. Memorize your agenda.

5. More is not better.

6. No eleventh-hour changes.

7. Envision the complete meeting.

8. Avoid doing anything weird, different, or wacky the night before or the morning of the presentation.

Work alone.

Prepare it yourself. Organize it your own way. Don't have someone put it together for you unless you have personally explained to him exactly what you want. Too often executives will have presentations organized by their staff. The result is a stilted delivery or, worse, a fake going-through-the-motions delivery. It's not your words, so you won't sound natural. It's not your outline, so it won't flow naturally. Your lack of participation translates to a lack of dedication. Your presentation will ring hollow.

Keep in mind that it's your reputation, your message, and your company that's on the line here. So be selfish and take time to be by yourself, work by yourself, and get it together on your own. An additional side benefit is that, just like a skydiver who packs her own parachute, you can be sure it's been done right.

Practice makes a master.

Practice works. It may seem an obvious truth, but it's so important it has to be said anyway. Practicing a golf swing, basketball layup, or the script in a play makes you better at execution, right? It's the same with a presentation. Practice makes you familiar with the content of your message—prices, schedules, competition, logistics, or whatever that content happens to be. The more familiar you are with your content, the more you can concentrate on your delivery. Murphy does everything he can to throw you off your game, especially at the start of a meeting. The clearer you are on your exact content and the sequence that your presentation will follow, the easier it is to anticipate Murphy and gracefully derail him.

Sales presentations are like telling a story, with you as the storyteller. Break down your presentation into invisible chapters. Practice revealing each chapter. Know the segues from one chapter to the next. Are the segues logical? Does your presentation excite you? Is it convincing? *Is it a book you'd read or would you put it back on the shelf?* Answer these essential questions and you'll alleviate self-doubt. And, lest we forget, self-doubt is where Murphy likes to hang his hat.

Know the objections you'll get.

When I'm in the field with a salesperson, I often notice clients raising questions or objections that the salesperson can't answer or resolve. That's okay, of course. We can't know everything. Yet, during the sales call's postmortem between the salesperson and me, he will often explain, "I knew the answer, but I didn't think of it at the time," or "I guess I didn't understand the question." Determining what kind of objections you may encounter plays a big part in controlling the sales call and controlling the eventual sale. When confused, ask a question or two to pinpoint the exact specific objection. Don't let it slide.

If your mind goes blank when asked a question that you believe you know the answer to, then just honestly answer, "For some reason or other, that answer has slipped my mind. Just give me a minute, and I'm sure I'll recall it." If it still doesn't come to you, promise to get back to the client with the answer as soon as possible.

Whatever you do, don't ignore a client's question. If you do, then count on the client asking the same question again a week later or, worse, losing the client because you appear detached and uninterested. And, yes, Murphy will have won. (For more information on dealing with questions and objections, see Chapter 9.)

Memorize your agenda.

> John, I was thinking about our meeting this past week, and I realized that it was essential to ask you several questions about your marketing objectives and to verify your competitive set before I make the linkage between you and my organization. I thought that I would resolve these questions, go into my recommendation, resolve questions that you or I may have, and finish up in about 40 minutes. Is that okay with you?

If you were the client how would you feel? You'd probably feel taken care of, because someone has engineered the meeting with a clear beginning, middle, and end. And someone volunteered to run the meeting: you!

Memorize your agenda and deliver it right after the handshake and some small talk. It sets the tone, the pace, and the parameters of the meeting, and it keeps you in control.

More is not better.

Far too often salespeople will pack 42 facts into a 12-fact presentation. Avoid this. It slows down your enthusiasm and puts clients to sleep. Don't misunderstand me. I am not recommending that you leave out salient data. What I am recommending is that you respect your client's time and the message that you are about to deliver. Carefully select the data that needs to be part of your message and add nothing more. Extra data is sometimes used as a security blanket, included to make you feel better as you "flex" your knowledge. Resist the temptation. Data should only be used to answer the exact goals of your client and nothing more.

No eleventh-hour changes.

The more changes you make as the meeting gets closer, the more you invite Murphy to come in and slime up things! With the exception of important late-breaking information (the stock of your client's organization crashed at the ring of yesterday's bell), have your presentation wrapped up a full day in advance. Spend those last hours practicing, not cramming.

Envision the complete meeting.

I am not talking here about a transcendental state—you know, candles, incense, mantra, Shirley McLain. I am speaking about visualizing your client hearing your story, assimilating it, and agreeing with your conclusions. This isn't hokey, it's sourcing your outcome—seeing your presentation come into existence, get accepted, and become the source of your desired outcome.

Think about what you want from the presentation. Now visualize it. If you see it in your mind first, it makes it easier to bring it to reality. By the way, if you can't visualize it in your mind, how on earth do you expect it to happen for real?

Avoid doing anything weird, different, or wacky the night before or the morning of the presentation.

If it's noticeably out of your ordinary routine—doing cartwheels with strips of bacon wrapped around each ear when normally you'd only be doing headstands—then don't do it the day or hours before a presentation. But wacky or weird is not only about skipping the far out, it's about anything out of the ordinary.

- Don't fast if you don't regularly fast.

- Don't overeat if you seldom overeat.

- Don't exercise to the point of exhaustion to relax your nerves.

- Don't stay late at the office cramming for the meeting.

- Don't crowd your schedule with appointments before your meeting.

- Don't arrive an hour before your meeting time.

- Don't arrive 1 minute before your meeting time (10 to 15 minutes is comfortable).

- Don't wear shoes that haven't been broken in.

- Don't use a new medium (such as changing from a paper presentation to a laptop presentation when you've never given a laptop presentation).

STEVE BUSTS MURPHY

One of the biggest mistakes you can make is overwhelming yourself in the minutia and leaving yourself little time for more important, overarching issues. In order to be ready for anything, you need to have a general presentation about your product that clearly, concisely, and preemptively answers just about any client's general questions. Think through the natural questions clients have before they engage you about your product and succinctly respond to those potential questions in your presentation.

The benefit of having a presentation that covers the basics about your product is that you do not have to reinvent the wheel each time you meet with a prospective client: You've already done the work. Clients will still ask difficult questions, of course. You can't know everything, so don't try. When a question arises that requires more time for you to answer, just tell the client that you will research this question and call her back with the answer the next morning. (And always get back to the client. Always!)

BOTTOM LINE

Concentrate on having a broad knowledge of the subject at hand. You'll be surprised how far that will go to answering most questions. Don't sweat knowing every little detail about everything (this doesn't apply to client

reconnaissance, of course). It can't be done, so don't
waste your energy trying.

FOUR KEYS TO KEEPING YOUR COOL

MURPHY STRIKES

In the middle of a recent one-on-one meeting, my new
client suddenly dropped a racist "joke," and I froze. He
laughed enough for both of us, so I'm sure he thought it
was funny, but I just found it offensive. It killed whatever
motivation I had to engage the man, and the sales call
ended shortly thereafter. What should I have done?

You've got worries, and you've got butterflies, but don't forget
your overarching goal: You're there to deliver your message.
Between that desire and achievement of your mission, however,
are plenty of places for pitfalls. To keep out of Murphy's way
during your sales meeting, rely on these four coolers to help
you through the rough spots.

1. Be your favorite teacher.

2. Don't take it personally.

3. Be flexible.

4. Maintain enthusiasm.

Be your favorite teacher.

Selling is nothing more than clear communication, the sharing of a clear thought. Think back to your school days and

your favorite teacher. The person who likely comes to mind is someone who taught you by making important lessons crystal clear.

For me it was my high school teacher Ms. Lynn. She was—as the old commercial used to say—cool, calm, collected. Nothing rattled her, and, believe me, we tried. Her communication style was always clear, concise, and insightful, and her reasoning always sound and logical. Often when I sell, I try to teach in her image, maintaining her clarity and passion for getting her message through regardless of the shenanigans or distractions. It always works.

Your favorite teacher might not have been a professional teacher, but a coach or a relative or neighbor. Whoever it was, determine the adjectives that best describe that person—dedicated, unflappable, spirited. Adapt those qualities to your own personal style, from your opening handshake to your parting one.

Don't take it personally.

Customers and clients are funny people. Unlike you and I, people who are perfectly normal in every way, they tend to come from left field when you least expect it. And when you do expect it, they're coming straight down the center. They have selective memory. They say things they mean and that they don't mean. Sometimes they love you and sometimes they . . . well, hate is such an ugly word. Let's move on to the main point here.

This isn't about you. It's about them. Put yourself out of the personality equation. Your job is to determine where they are on the "Richter scale" at any given moment and react in a way that keeps your message coming on strong.

How? First, remain neutral and objective. Second, as you'll discover throughout this book, the key to the kingdom of selling is asking the right questions at the right times. In this case, when clients get upset or say things that make you feel like you've got a glass jaw, compose yourself and ask a question to further understand their point of view or frame of reference. If you can't get into that state of mind, you can't resolve the problem. There will be no sale until you completely understand the problem.

When you take a comment or question personally, Murphy wins—big time. Taking it personally marks you as defensive and selfish, among the worst characteristics for a salesperson. When a client has an issue with something you said or presented and you get a negative reaction, just remain composed enough to read the situation objectively and slow the conversation down long enough to pinpoint the specific problem and what's making them so bent out of shape. Then resolve that problem.

As in other critical times of making sure you don't blow it, the key is to take the focus off yourself and put it where it belongs, in this case resolving your client's problem.

Be flexible.

Sometimes clients go off on tangents. Sometimes they want to talk about last night's failed soufflé, the home team's winning streak, or the cost of shampoo. Whatever it is, it's important to be flexible when it's appropriate to be flexible.

That means having the ability to take a presentation detour for a few minutes when your instinct says your client needs to be on that tangent. Being flexible sometimes means rescheduling your appointment in case of an emergency. You don't have to agree (having to drop off the Mercedes to get it detailed before the weekend perhaps doesn't strike you as an emergency). But you do have to remain flexible. Remaining flexible proves you are a good listener, someone who responds to needs, someone prepared and strong enough to handle small setbacks to advance a much bigger agenda.

Always factor in the possibility of surprise problems and pressures that may arise with your client and be ready to deal with them in a consultative, calm way.

Maintain enthusiasm.

This is not always easy to do. It's metaphorically similar to a boxer staying on the balls of his feet for the entire 3 minutes of a round. It takes stamina. It takes courage. It takes insight. It takes pride. Maintaining enthusiasm throughout a sales call does not mean being happy-go-lucky regardless of the conversation. It means holding oneself in an enthusiastic manner even when the going gets tough in the conversation.

How? Continually look for how you can achieve a partnership with your client even when a partnership doesn't seem possible. Challenge yourself and stay alert and on point. Watch for opportunity. When it appears, you'll be ready.

STEVE BUSTS MURPHY

Sometimes it's not you, but your client that shakes your cool. A bigoted joke or a tasteless remark can sour even the best of meetings. But, during any sales call always remember: never take it personally. In sales you've got to know when to get emotional and when to remain neutral and let things go, for the larger goal. Choose your battles carefully.

Sales is about understanding people and their motivations—starting with the realization that every client and potential client is different than you, has a different past than you, a different outlook. Generally speaking, that's great. Our differences make the world a challenging and interesting place. It also means that you're going to run into a class-A jerk now and then, as seems to be the case here. But, no matter who you're dealing with, if you look for someone to meet your expectations, count on being disappointed most of the time. Your client threw you a whammy. When that happens, regain control of the meeting by going back to the agenda that you set at the beginning of the meeting and state aloud where you are in relation to it ("Okay, we still need to determine a delivery schedule for the spring line.") and restart the sales call.

BOTTOM LINE

Don't hold your client to your standards. Don't get sidelined for anything, not for a sour remark, not a stupid and insensitive story, nothing. Concentrate on the sale.

PERSIST THROUGH GAFFES

MURPHY STRIKES

A couple of years back, I stood up to make a point and dipped my tie full square into my coffee. Tie dripping, I couldn't decide if I should take it off, squeeze it into the cup and continue, or what. My face was red, my white shirt coffee-brown, and the presentation ruined. Was it possible to rescue this situation?

As you prepare for your meeting, imagine that CNN will be there broadcasting it live. How's that make you feel? Nervous? Worried? Self-conscious?

It should not make any difference at all. Facing your next meeting as though it's going out live to the world lets you take the bull by the horns: Come what may, you're going to prevail regardless of any possible mistakes.

But, gaffes or blunders come in many forms. And Murphy is never caught without one. So, what can you do?

It depends on the gaffe, of course, but the general rule is to take responsibility for the mistake and recommend that the presentation move on.

If you're anxious before a meeting, an old theater rule is to go to the restroom and compose yourself for a few minutes before entering the client's office. Take several deep breaths. Reflect on the efforts you've made up until now to get to the point of having a meeting. Reflect on your understanding of your client's situation, on the genuine linkage between what you will recommend and what your client needs. Reflect upon other clients you've helped who are in a similar situation.

These reflections will give you the courage to carry yourself with pride and determination. So, now you're steeled to go into the meeting with confidence. But what happens when Murphy makes an appearance during the presentation? Listed below are several steps to take to minimize possible gaffes:

- Use the facilities before your meeting, not only to put your thoughts together, but also to minimize any physical distractions you may encounter during the presentation.

- Be prepared to meet five new listeners for the presentation you expected to deliver to just one. I know, the client said, "Don't worry, it will just be you and me next week." What you don't know is that during the week five other executives expressed interest in your upcoming meeting and now want to hear what you have to say firsthand. Be flattered and step up to bat.

- Have your schedule and a calendar handy and know, just in case, when you can meet your client again. When the client comes out of the office and says something urgent came up and so she just can't make it today, be ready to reschedule. Sometimes the excuse is legitimate and sometimes it's a lie. The excuse is not your worry. Your job is to be persistent and achieve your basic goal: Have that meeting.

- If at all possible, ask that the meeting be held in a conference room, not your client's office. Murphy has more ammunition in the client's office. Think about it: People know where your client's office is, but they probably don't know which conference room he'll choose. The client's phone and cell phone are back in the office, not in the conference room. The client's computer is in the office, not in the conference room. The client is more easily distracted in his own office (that's where he keeps little knick-knacks that he loves to play with). Finally, the meeting room is a more neutral playing field, unlike the office which is really the client's personal domain and where you are simply a visitor.

- Get to the conference room beforehand to set up. I can't begin to count the number of times I have rearranged a conference room, single-handedly, in order to maintain control of the meeting. Often there are too many chairs, the room is a mess, or there's not enough presentation room to illustrate the graphics that I'll be using. Make the space conducive to your message; it makes a difference. If you see a phone in the room and your client has a history of taking phone calls during your meeting, disconnect the phone. Dirty pool? No. Someone who isn't giving you his full attention during a meeting is the one playing dirty pool. You'll reconnect the phone when you leave. Your message deserves his full, undivided attention.

- Place your water or coffee away from you and your papers to avoid knocking them over. Yes, it's happened to me; that's why I'm giving you this advice. (By the way, if you're offered water or coffee and you accept, you have to drink it. It's a matter of being respectful.) If given the choice of water or coffee, go with water, especially if you speak a lot. If you walk into a meeting a little anxious, trust me, you don't need any more stimulants.

- Be calm with your movements. Too many salespeople make too many unnecessary movements. This communicates one thing, and one thing only: nerves. We've discussed the importance of practicing. If you've practiced this meeting, you have also choreographed what visual aids you'll be using and in what order. Don't stand there like a zombie, but remember you're making a presentation, not landing a jumbo jet at O'Hare.

- Be neat with your paperwork and presentation materials. Don't get caught pulling excess papers and booklets from your briefcase. Neatness counts—trite, but true. Be measured and matter-of-fact with presentation material. Too many disconnected papers indicate that you're disconnected and not secure in your message.

- Don't interrupt. Even when you catch yourself with your mouth open ready to interrupt your client and you don't say anything, they know that you are onto your next thought and not focusing on theirs. An urge to interrupt means you're not listening.

STEVE BUSTS MURPHY

Now, what about our friend who used his necktie as a coffee stir stick? Can a situation like this be rescued? This one has "emergency" written all over it, but, yes, it is possible—if you approach the problem with grace and charm. Try these steps:

1. Laugh at it. (I mean, come on now! You must have looked pretty funny!) This gives your clients a chance to laugh too and takes the tension and embarrassment out of the air.

2. Like Dean Martin slipping off his bow tie to break into a standard, carefully remove your tie, fold it, and announce with a smile that the next stop is the dry

cleaners. (In your head, however, promise yourself that if you're able to turn this gaffe into a profitable meeting, you'll go to Saks Fifth Avenue and get yourself a new tie.)

3. Button your jacket and cover that caffeinated map of Asia now spreading across your white shirt.

4. Bring the meeting back to focus by restating the agenda and what step you are about to take. Ask the clients if they agree. After they nod, proceed.

5. Take your soggy, coffee-soaked presentation and throw it away. That's right, throw it away. Then reach into your briefcase and take out your backup copy that you always carry. In fact, have three copies. One for backup and one to give to the client in case she's so excited about your presentation she wants to share it with her boss right away. And it will also be handy should a colleague of the client want to sit in on the meeting. They'll be able to follow along and will be impressed that you were prepared.

BOTTOM LINE

Mistakes are human. When one happens to you, act like a human. If it's funny, acknowledge it with a little laugh. This keeps your feet planted firmly in reality (after all, it's only a stained tie—perspective, folks!) and gives you the ability to move forward with assurance.

CHAPTER

4

SOUL SEARCHING

WHO, BESIDES MURPHY, WILL SEE YOU?

About a year ago I was hired to coach a sales executive on many areas of his game. But I soon discovered that his biggest stumbling block occurred long before he even had a chance to get his foot in the door. In fact, it was getting his foot in the door that was the problem.

His challenge was personified by the head of a major beauty care company. My salesman knew his product was good and he was clear on the message, but he was bedeviled with self-doubt about his chances to even get a meeting, much less present his case.

The traditional way to deal with issues of self-doubt would be to convince the salesperson that he just needs to have the moxie to go knock on the door and get that meeting. If you come to me expecting that, you will be disappointed.

My job is to give people tools to overcome their difficulties in their careers as salespeople. I am not a booster, a cheerleader, or a guy who thinks the solution to such problems is a pep talk. What I tell people may motivate them, but I am not a motivational speaker. I'm given real problems, and it's my job to deliver real solutions. Attempting to help this person overcome his doubts about getting a meeting by boosting his ego ("You can do it!") would be like my father telling a sick patient, "Just wish that appendicitis away!"

What this guy needed, and what I recommended, was knowledge about his potential client. We scoured the company's Web site, its annual report, and other documents and determined its marketing goals. Then the salesman looked at what he had to offer this company that would specifically speak to its marketing goals. This "match" was the key to tailoring his phone canvas to convince the executive that what the salesperson had to share was worth seeing in person.

Clients don't want to see you to help you. They want to see you to help themselves.

Having something that the customer wants and needs is the key to gaining the one-on-one interview. When you call to offer an answer to that want or need, you are taking the first step in your business relationship—a step that directly leads to a fruitful relationship.

Think about it. When you call to say you'd like to show the client a product or service that will directly speak to the company's objectives, you're starting on a path focused on what will help the client. This has to be at the center of your efforts throughout the selling process, so you might as well begin now.

THREE QUESTIONS YOU MUST ASK YOURSELF BEFORE YOUR FIRST PHONE CALL

MURPHY STRIKES

I'm generally a friendly person, but when I start off that way on a phone call to get a meeting, it's sometimes hard to switch gears to the business at hand. What can I do?

There are three important issues you must resolve beyond any degree of doubt before you pick up the phone to call a potential client.

1. How am I memorable?
What sets you apart? Why is your product or service better than anyone else's? What advantages do you bring? This question forces you to uncover the core of who you are and why your product or service is worth sharing with the world. Sum up those answers in brief, easy-to-understand statements.

2. Am I prepared?
Do you know your product, your client, your client's competition? If you've prepared properly, you will uncover your

client's needs, make a meaningful pitch on the phone, and mutually determine the appropriateness of a face-to-face presentation (and, in the process, not waste your time or your client's), handle objections, and set in motion a successful sales relationship.

3. *What do I want to happen?*

Weight trainers tell clients to look in the mirror as they curl those dumbbells and imagine that they see growth in their biceps. It's not a mind game; it really helps to improve that specific muscle group. If you know what you want to happen and can imagine it, you have a much better shot at making it happen. What goal have you set for this meeting? It's a simple, but crucial question. When you call a client, know in your mind what you expect to happen when you meet the client. You must be ready to share that information with the client, so make sure that the expectations are ones that benefit the client.

STEVE BUSTS MURPHY

If you start out friendly and businesslike, there's no need to switch gears. There's a difference between being friendly and being someone's friend. After saying hello, state plainly why you are calling. Make a business connection about the client's needs (if you don't know before you call, you're jumping the gun) and do it in a friendly manner.

BOTTOM LINE

As long as your focus is on helping the client, your conversation will naturally be businesslike and friendly.

AIM HIGH, ONE STEP AT A TIME

MURPHY STRIKES

The preparation for my phone pitch was to talk to a secretary on how to arrange a meeting with the vice president of marketing. Having arrived at my office early one morning, I called (cold) my prospective client to leave a voice mail. I didn't get voice mail. I didn't get the secretary or the vice president; instead I got the CEO of the company itself, explaining that it was so early that he was one of the few people in the office at that hour to answer phones. Totally flummoxed, I said I'd call back later. What do I do when I get the big fish on the line when I'm angling for the small-fry?

Ever heard this one: "As your manager I'm telling you to get to the decision maker, the highest-ranking person there, and sell them first!" You may hear this often, but just because it's said a lot, does that mean it's right? Maybe yes, maybe no. You must eventually get to the highest-ranking person and sell them, yes! Is it always the way to go from the start? No.

Sales can be a fun chess game if you approach it that way. From your reconnaissance you always need to pinpoint the people that will be involved in deciding on your product long before you see anyone. This mapping of the "client chessboard" is paramount to determining whom to see and in what order to see them.

Meeting with the highest decision maker at the very start of a sales campaign can backfire if you are not aware of the food chain of that company. You need to understand how decisions are made at that company as they relate to your product. Invariably, there are anywhere from one to as many as seven different decision makers in any one company. Smart salespeople determine before their initial meeting who should be seen and in what order.

No two clients can ever be sold the same way. Seeing the highest-level person within an organization and asking them simple unsophisticated questions could ruin your chances of selling anything there for a year or more. Aiming too low could waste your time with people whose opinions carry little or no weight with the honchos. So the question becomes, How do we determine whom to see and what do we ask them when we get there?

Much of the decision rests on what reconnaissance you're able to perform. How much do you understand about the organization and who are the decision makers? If you get stuck completing your research, you may need to meet with an insider at your client's company (if that's possible) to put all the pieces together.

After you've determined whom you need to see, you must study a company and figure out what questions to ask. What questions you ask will reveal to your client your professional self and hard work.

Every person has a different connection point, a certain way that he or she needs to be spoken to and sold to. Your pitch must fit that connection point. With high-level decision makers, often it's best to find out about them from their direct reports. Asking specific questions about a key decision maker from the decision maker's direct reports gives you a great edge when eventually meeting them; it also keeps Murphy from turning your call into a party line.

It is also important to prioritize the meeting you will ask for. You need to determine who needs to be seen and in what order. This is critical to your image inside the company and your ability to eventually put the client puzzle together for your big meeting with the decision maker.

STEVE BUSTS MURPHY

You've determined the order of whom you need to see, but, by chance, the CEO answers the phone. Hey, it happens. I know a journalist who used to purposely place his calls very early in the morning on a business day, knowing that it was unlikely that the secretary of the CEO would be in, but that there was a good chance the boss would be. He said it was a good trick that often paid off.

If you aim to get a lower-level executive and just so happen to ring up the top dog, first thank the executive for picking up the phone ("It's great that the head of a company still sometimes answers the phone!") and explain to them the purpose of your call, whom you were trying to reach, and the idea you wanted to discuss with that person. Who knows, the CEO may push it along too!

BOTTOM LINE

Be ready for whoever answers the phone. If it happens to be the head of the company, state whom you were originally trying to reach, but share the basic thrust of your pitch. You may get a new advocate who can help your efforts along.

5

HEY! HOW YA DOIN'?

MAKING MURPHY-FREE SMALL TALK

A client of mine was stuck. He had an executive who would never say yes to his product and he couldn't get him to budge. My client asked if I would accompany him on a sales call for what he described as a "last chance" to get through to this executive.

Before the call, I insisted that together we study the company's Web site, 11 pages of news, product updates, and other company information. During our research we discovered that the Food and Drug Administration (FDA) was close to approving the spray form of a health and beauty aid that was a key product in the company's line.

When we arrived for our last-chance encounter, my client and I said hello and then immediately mentioned the government's pending approval by remarking, "So, when do you think the FDA will approve your best-selling medication in spray form, especially since Canada's already approved it?" The executive, clearly impressed, brightened up and asked, "How did you know that we were working on that exact issue yesterday?"

Sometimes it's not that Murphy goofs you up, it's that he won't even let you get your foot in the door by zapping you at the opening moments of the meeting.

My client got the sale in 2 weeks. The lesson is to make your opening statements intelligent, thoughtful, and pithy.

The moment you greet your client must be light, tight, and bright. This is the point in time, the seconds that follow the hello and handshake, to say something that proves you know the client's business, you're there in the spirit of good business, and you're neither a cold fish nor a best friend.

A FINE HOW-DO-YOU-DO

MURPHY STRIKES

Once I get going, I seem to do okay in my presentations, but starting is always tough for me. I never know if I should start with a joke, be serious, folksy, or what. What's a proven starter?

Your client's business needs must be an obvious concern of yours from the moment you say hello. You've done your reconnaissance; you've made the appointment. Now, you're ready to walk into the client's office and project an aura of ease, confidence, and care.

When the great Ozzie Smith, one of the most amazing short-stops in the history of baseball, was inducted into the Baseball Hall of Fame in January 2002, it was the week I was set to meet with Andy Hersam, director of New York advertising for *Sports Illustrated* magazine. I genuinely love baseball, and it is not much of a stretch for me to play the role of an enthusiast when I meet with someone who's professionally connected to sports.

I knew Andy's work kept him up on news such as the Hall of Fame inductees, so I mentioned my thrill about Smith's well-deserved recognition. I told him about the many mind-boggling plays I'd seen this phenomenon make on *Sports Illustrated*'s cable network, CNNSI. Andy listened to my comments and then began laughing. "Why are you laughing?" I asked. He replied, "You won't believe who I had dinner with last night." That's right, Ozzie Smith.

I was blown away by this coincidence. Andy explained that Ozzie called him up to arrange a dinner with *Sports Illustrated* personnel to thank them for all their support throughout his career. We talked for at least 10 minutes. It was an honest, convivial exchange about a subject truly appreciated.

Was the topic of conversation a coincidence? Even Murphy would have to say, "I think not."

It was natural, Murphy-free small talk tailored for the situation. I chose my opening subject matter precisely because I knew it related to the business, but also because it was something I knew so much about. The result was a natural link between my client's business and current events. That's it in a nutshell folks: *Draw a natural link between the client's business and current events.* This is the key to Murphy-free small talk.

Being successful with small talk is not a layup (I promise this will be the last of the sports metaphors, at least for this chapter). Solid, connected client small talk takes planning and forethought, as well as caring, friendliness, intelligence, and a reasonably good memory (you have to be able to recall which product in the client's line has recently been a hit in Asian markets, and which ones have flopped—a mix-up here only turns your opening remarks into a jumble).

You want a successful sales meeting? Get people talking. You see them with their guard let down. The more someone speaks to you, the more you see the person in three dimensions. You get a window—at least a peek—into people's likes and dislikes, how they decide issues, and their values. Understanding what clients hold dear and having a general idea as to their values eases communication.

Don't let Murphy stall you out in the first minutes of a sales call. Converse with your clients about issues that are meaningful to them.

An advertising salesperson I was working with had an appointment in New York with one of the world's largest advertising agencies. He was going to present his magazine as an advertising vehicle appropriate for one of the agency's big clients.

Upon arrival we ask if we can wait in the waiting room until our client is finished with her previous meeting. So we sit and wait. And wait. And wait.

Finally, the assistant media director surfaces. As she steps toward us to shake our hands she states flatly, "Sorry, I'm running late. I'll only have 10 minutes to meet with you. Things are crazy since I've moved back from London."

She might have been late but she was in control. My salesperson automatically replies, "Okay, I'll be quick." He then proceeded to ask two questions (he later explained that his probing had to be brief because he was so squeezed for time) and then launched into a not bad presentation of the different departments of his magazine.

The client politely listened, but at precisely the 10-minute mark she said, "Thanks for stopping in. Sorry, I really have to go now."

As we packed up our notes, I asked her, "Since moving from London, have you noticed that advertising people in the UK have more savvy than New York advertising people?" She immediately brightened up, relaxed her face and body, albeit for a moment, smiled, and said, "I can't believe you said that! That's the main thing I've noticed about this business since I returned from London!"

The ice was broken. Unfortunately, it was at the end of the meeting instead of the beginning. My salesperson should have engaged the client, asked how her return to New York was going, way before he said, "Okay, I'll be quick." He needed to be ready with some successful small talk. He needed to show caring and empathy, that he wasn't on autopilot, that he was, above all, *selfless enough to consider what was obviously uppermost on his client's mind.*

He needed to realize that moving from London to New York was causing trauma for the client—she had, after all, *just said it out loud*. Speak to the client's needs.

You can talk about anything in the opening minutes of the meeting, but avoid statements that immediately link to your goals in the meeting. One of the last things you want to say is something along the lines of "I hear your company's having a tough time in overseas markets, so I think you're going to like what I have to say about how we can help there!" Get your client talking *before* you talk about why you're there.

When I went with a salesperson in Los Angeles to see a client, we both noticed an 8 by 10, beautifully framed photograph of a man striking a soccer ball sitting on the client's desk. The salesperson (correctly) acknowledged the photograph and asked who the person was in the picture. Her client stated, with more than a little pride, that the subject was none other than her husband, currently a semipro soccer player in Los Angeles.

This would be known as a successful opening, and things were going quite well at this point. Then, all of a sudden, my salesperson launched into an unrestrained diatribe on her soccer past at Holy Cross College some 15 years ago. In case you don't get the level of boredom this might evoke, let me repeat: *her soccer past at college 15 years ago.* It lasted 2 to 3 minutes and seemed like an hour and a half. I watched as the life force of the client whooshed out of her face as she sat listening to my client discuss her many goals throughout her college sports career.

The salesperson was discussing a subject dear to the client. But, what was wrong with this small talk at the core? It's really quite simple. At the start of the meeting, masterful salespeople let clients talk more than they do. They gently lead their client to issues that are easy to comment on. They listen keenly for topics that will lead to more friendly, honest discussion that lets the client open up.

I observed a salesperson in New York meeting with a client for the first time. As the meeting began, we discussed sports from the past weekend's games on TV. The salesperson I was observing was knowledgeable about sports, too knowledgeable. My salesperson was busy recalling the latest matchup between two West Coast teams—great recall—but he forgot to let the client talk more than him.

I decided to chime in. I asked the client if he had a favorite hockey team. He brightened up 100 percent, threw out a big smile and said, "I'm from Philadelphia, and I love the Philadelphia Flyers. I have all my life."

Here was the doorway my salesperson needed to pick up the hint and begin to discuss the current record of the Flyers, their past, their prospects for the coming season, *something* connected to continue the small talk phase of our meeting. But instead, upon hearing the client's exuberance about the Flyers, my salesperson began flipping through the magazine he represented and selected an article. He proceeded to show the article to the client by saying, "I think you'll find this really interesting about the Detroit Red Wings!"

I caught myself and closed my gaping mouth. I was shocked that my salesperson could be that insensitive about the Flyers and his client's adoration for them—and I watched the client's face and smile drop the moment the salesperson offered the article to him.

There are times when you'll want to show a client something that you think is a plausible link to your immediate conversation. Sometimes it'll work and sometimes it won't, but how can you be sure?

Hold off on any show-and-tell until your client's fervor for a subject has been fully communicated and realized. This shows your selflessness and gives you a window into the personality of your client, a valuable piece of information and a very precious thing.

STEVE BUSTS MURPHY

There is no single pat expression that works every time with every client. The best conversational ice-breaker for a business meeting is to mention an aspect of the client's industry that is topical and important, maybe something that's been in the news lately. For example, you might begin with, "I noticed in the *Wall Street Journal* yesterday that your company's European operations are going to cut back personnel by 10 percent. Has it had an impact with your work here?" Alternatively, you could ask, "Your annual report presents a pretty aggressive strategy for the coming year. How's that going to affect your department?" State one or two aspects of an issue, ask for your client's thoughts on the matter, and then sit back and listen. Opening with an informed insight shows knowledge of your client's world, knowledge that your client may not figure you have and which is, therefore, impressive. And it can be accomplished in the first 30 seconds of a meeting.

BOTTOM LINE

Use a topical, business-oriented statement or question to open conversation and show your genuine interest in your client and the client's company.

LIKE YOUR HAIR. HOPE IT WINS.

MURPHY STRIKES

I went into my meeting feeling my normal level of friendliness, but when I saw his snakeskin boots I immediately flashed on the pair I had in college and felt an instant consanguinity. When I expressed genuine enthusiasm about how much I liked his boots, he responded, "Wow, I guess you really do want this sale." It deflated me to have my true emotions equated with monetary pursuit. I sheepishly insisted that I really liked the boots, but it left me cold. What do you do when the client takes the wind out of your sails on the opening remark?

Years ago I was watching a boy on television who claimed the title of World Yo-Yo Champion. As he performed his various stunts, he would announce the name of each, "walk the dog," "around the world," and so on. During one intricate maneuver, he fumbled the string and the trick spectacularly flopped. "That's the easiest one of all," the boy calmly announced. "It's called 'The Mistake.'"

Nothing is easier than making an error. We're all human, we have all done it, and most of the time you can usually handle a simple faux pas with a good-natured remark and move on. But, when the mistake is made at the opening phrase, it's much tougher to recover because it means your initial introduction has fallen flat and that puts pressure on everything else.

The best way to avoid conversation killers is to never bring them up. Some remarks are obviously out of place. We've all heard the warnings about never discussing religion or politics at dinner, and that certainly applies during a sales call—especially for your opening remarks. You just can't assume that your client has similar beliefs to yours. Similarly, you would never make a remark about someone's race, sexual orientation, religion, or nationality. It's just plain rude. Never tell a joke that's at another's expense.

Okay, so those are the obvious ones. Other remarks, however, are not so easy to pinpoint. You must remember that you make a sales call to expand the possibilities (create a better business relationship, achieve new or increased sales, become more knowledgeable about your client), so make sure that your remarks help in that growth, not limit it.

Here are a few simple rules:

1. Don't flatter the client, especially a woman. "I like your hairdo" says you've got your mind on her looks, not her business needs.

2. Never make a negative comment on someone's clothing. "Wow! That's a wild tie!" is akin to saying, "Who dressed you?"

3. Never talk about yourself for too long. If a client notices your tan and asks if you just returned from vacation, and you actually did, mention where you were and immediately ask about her vacation plans this year.

4. Get off subjects that your instinct says are not fun for your client (he could care less that the circus is in town).

5. Don't engage in sports talk unless the client brings it up or you've asked if sports are an interest.

6. Avoid any declaration of anything you have a strong opinion on until you have a sense of where your client will come out on that issue.

7. Don't use even mildly off-color language. Avoid statements such as, "Boy, these guys really bust your hump don't they?" or "I got screwed out of a great parking space coming here."

STEVE BUSTS MURPHY

You made a genuine compliment on your client's boots and he took it as you trying to butter him up? *Laugh at it!* Explain why you like the boots and what they reminded you of. That's a great start to a meeting. Tell him how the boots brought you back to a great time in your life. However he may want to distort your statement, you are still telling the truth for you, and that's what counts. He's left with his ridiculous, inappropriate judgment, made either to test you or to illustrate his jadedness toward life in general. It's certainly not about you—he doesn't even know you.

As we say in Brooklyn, "fugettaboudit." Move off it and articulate your agenda to the meeting. But, watch this guy. Are his responses brief? Does he show a lack of connectedness to your questions and ideas? If you notice these, restate the purpose of the meeting and get his agreement to move forward. This action says to your client, "No more games. Are you serious or not?"

BOTTOM LINE

A negative reaction to a genuine, appropriate compliment is an indication of a larger problem with the client. Look for other indications of distance from your message. Bring the client back to the proper focus on what the meeting offers.

CHAPTER

6

SET THE AGENDA
TAKE CONTROL
FROM MURPHY

"I don't have much time" is among the most commonly heard phrases. It's true, of course, since all of us usually keep too many irons in the fire and time is always running short. Still, it takes on added significance when it's the first words out of a client's mouth at the beginning of a meeting.

On one of my technique observation trips with a new salesperson, the client greeted us in his office by bluntly telling us, "I don't have much time" while we were shaking hands. When my salesperson eagerly replied, "Okay, then let's get started!" I assumed he was ready to take the bull by the horns.

Instead, he launched into his regular spiel. At 10 minutes, the client was looking at his watch in a way that physically underscored his earlier words. I noticed that the new sales-person saw what I saw, so I figured he'd pick up on it and change his approach. No. He simply said, "I've just got a few more facts." At 15 minutes, the client, fidgeting, remarked that time was elapsing. Now the client was sending a message in words and body language. Again, the salesperson blew it, saying, "I'll just discuss a few more points." At 20 minutes (that seemed infinitely longer thanks to the edgy nature of the meeting), the client said he needed to leave, to which the salesperson explained that he was almost done. Almost done? I was thinking, "No, Pal. You're finished."

Then the client stood up and emphatically announced, "No, I need to leave now!" With that, he gathered a few papers from his desk, said he was sure we could find our way out on our own, and left his office.

I always follow up meetings like this by debriefing the salesperson on what went right and what went wrong. As you can imagine, the "what went wrong" part was pretty intense. But, of all the errors that this new salesperson made, the biggest was that he didn't get everyone to agree, at the begin-ning of the meeting, how much time was available.

"I don't have much time," may be a fact, but it's an unknown quantity. If my salesperson had nailed it down to minutes—"I'm sorry you're rushed. How much time can you spare?"—he could have turned the meeting to his advantage by determining exactly how much he could reasonably accomplish in the 5, 10, 15, or 20 minutes available. He could then state, briefly, the agenda for the given time span, and then arrange a time for the next meeting to complete the

task at hand. He stays in control of the time, even when it's squeezed.

Many factors come into play at a sales meeting, and it's impossible to control them all. But, one you can control is the agenda. By stating clearly at the beginning of the meeting exactly what you intend to do and how long the process will take—and then getting agreement to your stated objectives—you command the situation and stay in charge of the meeting.

LAY IT ON THE LINE

MURPHY STRIKES
Explaining to the client at the beginning of the meeting that I'd like to take 30 or 40 minutes makes even me cringe at what seems like a long, long time. Couldn't I just promise that it won't take more than "a few minutes" and then let my—believe me on this one—fascinating presentation extend the meeting to as long as necessary to bowl my client over?

If you state your agenda clearly at the beginning of a meeting and have the client agree to your outline, the meeting can proceed without any unpleasant surprises. For instance, if your clients know that you want to start by asking some questions to get to know more about their business, they will be much more ready to answer what you need to know.

The benefit of articulating an agenda right after your opening small talk is that you respectfully take control of the sales call. Remember, clients don't agree to see you because they want to make a new friend. They have an agenda in mind before you get there. They want to know the price of your product (and usually within the first 30 seconds of your meeting), when you can deliver your service, the specific differences from your product versus the one they've been using for 10 years, or answers to a host of other questions. You need to deliver this information, but at the right time. Unless you set the agenda, you don't control the sales call. That means you leave it to the client to control the sales call; in other words, you let Murphy control it. As a salesperson you must commit to controlling the sales call, and that requires an agenda.

Craft the agenda to a sales call the day before the call. Write the agenda down and study it. Put yourself in your client's shoes and decide if the agenda that you've crafted makes good business sense.

The agenda must respectfully manage the client's wants and needs, taking into regard both your time frame and the client's, and simultaneously facilitate a quality meeting. The agenda you put forth will do that. A tight, clear agenda communicates knowledge, empathy, and structure. Clients like that. Murphy hates it.

Clients are impressed with salespeople who come to meetings prepared to put forth an agenda that takes their issues into account along with the salesperson's issues. Clients enjoy being led, provided it's done respectfully not selfishly. Recommend your agenda, but don't demand it. If you have crafted your agenda to take the client's issues into account, you will gain their agreement.

You must gain the client's willing agreement to your agenda. You need to ask clients if your agenda is okay with them. Their agreement says, "Yes, it's okay with me that you handle our meeting." This is a key point in controlling your meeting. Without it you've got a tug-of-war with Murphy at the front of your rope.

So much could be going through the mind of your client, it's hard to tell at the start of a call where they might be coming from. That's the very reason why you must offer an agenda, to put your clients at ease (it lets them know their issues will be the focus of your meeting) and put you in control.

Before my father operated on a patient, he would outline exactly what he was going to do, essentially explaining the agenda of the operation. He would carefully explain the specific goal of the operation and the steps it would take, from opening incision to the patient's expected recovery time. As he put forth the operation's agenda he would always look right at his patient, watching facial expressions and sensing his or her level of understanding of his words. He knew when to review a specific point of the operation and when to move on. He also had a priceless way of being uplifting throughout his delivery.

At the beginning of the meeting, embody that delivery style when you present your agenda: confident, careful, caring. If you force the delivery, you can count on your client resisting your agenda. This isn't *Dragnet*, and you're not Joe Friday. At the other end of the spectrum, don't be tentative with your delivery. You have knowledge to share. Let that show.

One issue you must determine is whether you will simply state your agenda or present it in written form. This will usually depend on the number of people attending the meeting. When you meet with one to two clients, you only need to speak your agenda as you are about to begin. It's more informal and conversational. Meeting with three or more people requires more formality, so the content of your meeting should show that. Before the beginning of the meeting, have written time guidelines on how you expect the meeting to proceed.

This means, however, that you will need to contact the lead client the day before and get an agreement on the agenda beforehand. Then, if you can, clear it with each participant. Once you've gotten agreement, write out your agenda and have it at each person's place at the table as they take their seats. This shows you are prepared and professional.

When you speak your agenda, here's how it should sound:

Jane, yesterday I was thinking about this meeting and I realized that there were several questions that are important to resolve with regard to your overall marketing goals and direction for this year. Once these questions are answered, then I'll be able to make the linkage that we discussed over the phone between your company and ours, and we'll finish up with any questions that you and I have of one another. We should be done in about 40 minutes. Is that okay?

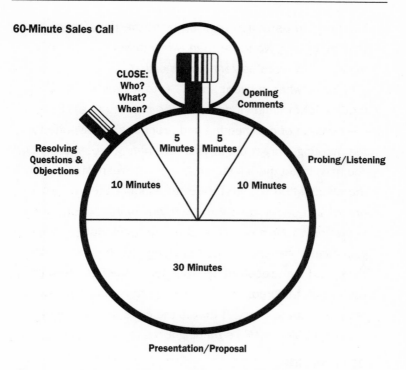

This stopwatch offers a minute-by-minute guide on how to apportion your time during a 60-minute meeting.

In this case, you've respectfully put forth an agenda that takes control of the meeting right from the start.

STEVE BUSTS MURPHY

You feel more comfortable asking for "a few minutes" rather than plainly stating that what the meeting will really require is 30 to 40 minutes? This is a problem. For starters it's a lie. But, beyond the fact that you're being dishonest, you're shortchanging yourself.

You need to establish right up front the importance of your meeting. "No more than a few minutes" is a food delivery, not a professional sales call.

I like it when a client says "30 to 40 minutes—wow that's a lot of time!" It gives me the opening to establish the purpose of our meeting and articulate the agenda to the meeting. Forget about your fascinating presentation. You have to get there first. What about the respect you owe the client when you first meet to conduct the interview process to understand if there is any need for your presentation? Your meeting is about understanding whom your clients are, the issues thwarting their business success, and then resolving these issues together. The way you've got it figured, the meeting's purpose is your show, not the client's. Sorry! If that is the case, turn the meeting over to Murphy. He's running it now.

BOTTOM LINE

Be honest about the amount of time you need for your meeting. Remind clients—and yourself—that it takes time to serve their needs and help in their success.

AS IF YOU HAD NOTHING BETTER TO DO

MURPHY STRIKES

I'm always on time, so I find it particularly galling when I'm made to wait for a scheduled meeting. My recent situation with a new client left me really steaming.

> After being made to wait for 30 minutes, the client's sec-
> retary came out and told me, "He's really sorry but he
> won't be able to make it today. If you leave your card,
> we'll call you back to reschedule." I practically yelled, "No
> need to bother!" and stormed out of there. Was I right, or
> should I have just bit my lip and rolled with it?

I've said it before and will again, but it's especially important to remember when you've been made to wait an inordinate amount of time for a meeting: Don't take it personally. Anytime you expect someone to behave a certain way, you set yourself up for disappointment. Drop the expectations and you drop the disappointment. It's not easy, but it's better than tearing your hair out.

One of the many sayings attributed to Confucius is, "To one who waits, a moment is like eternity." You're sitting on the waiting room couch, irritated by the harsh glow of the florescent lights, and noticing everything from the dust on the plastic ivy in the planter to the cigarette burn hole in the shag carpet. And that's just in the first 5 minutes.

As the time drags on to 10, 15, 20 minutes or more, you're going through a gamut of emotions and questions: Are you such a low priority to this client? What will this do to the rest of your day's schedule? Will you get your full meeting time or be squeezed? How dare someone treat you like this! Are they really busy or just putting you off?

You know not to take it personally, but it is, after all, you who are being made to wait and that's pretty personal. So how can you change the focus? The best way I've found is to manage your waiting time correctly. Go through your notes on the upcoming meeting. Review notes for meetings later that day or the next day. Check your calendar for times you'll be available should you need to reschedule.

Keep track of the time. After 10 minutes, ask to speak to your client's administrative assistant and ask if everything is okay with your meeting. The response will probably be something along the lines of "Oh, she's just finishing up another meeting," or "His conference call is running long, but he's almost done." Just as an attorney objects in a trial to prove a point to the jury, whether overruled or sustained, the point is made. So, too, have you proven your point, that you are not to be taken for granted.

At 20 minutes you need to consider the possibility that the meeting will be canceled. Ask the administrative assistant, "Do you keep his calendar? Do you know when her next meeting is?" If there is no meeting following close on the heels of yours, relax and wait. When you do meet, the client will owe you.

If you find that the client's next meeting will drastically cut into your time, pull out your electronic organizer or day planner and ask the assistant if it's possible to reschedule for later that day or week. Be flexible.

Sure, you've decided to wait. Once the client has arrived and greets you, *always* make a comment on the time, *but don't do it with malice; do it with empathy*. If you choose to not comment on the lateness, your action indicates you agree with the lateness. If you comment with malice, kiss your meeting and that relationship good-bye.

By commenting with empathy, you nicely let the client know that the action was noticed, but you are ready to move on.

John, how are you? Thanks for the time to reflect on our meeting. I was able to review some questions that I realized needed some resolution before we get into the heart of our meeting.

You've noted the tardiness, but you're keeping it positive. Always reconfirm the time you have for your meeting at the start of your meeting.

It's now 10:20 a.m., let's meet until 11:00 a.m., how's that?

These statements are essential to controlling your meeting. Even if he says, "Oh, wow, but I've only got 20 minutes," you will at least have drawn first blood by nicely stating that you were able to determine several essential questions that needed to be addressed before beginning your sales pitch and you recommended a specific time frame to complete your meeting. So, before he says he only has 10 minutes he's heard you say that for the meeting to be meaningful and thorough it will require 40 minutes.

Once he says he only has 10 minutes he has countermanded your empathetic position by taking a selfish position. After the client says he only has 10 minutes, recommend that you schedule a time to complete the meeting at some point next week.

It should sound like this (said with a smile):

John, in order to complete our agenda, we should meet for the 40 minutes we discussed on the phone. Let's meet for as much time as we can now and then schedule the balance of time we both determine we need to complete our meeting. How's that?

He now knows you care and that the next step needs to be rescheduling the balance of the time that originally was agreed upon. And, you have said so in a very empathetic way. You have countered his counteroffer (10 minutes) and trial closed him on it. It may sound like an army maneuver or a wrestling move, but it's neither. It's thorough, smart, empathetic, and in-control selling.

STEVE BUSTS MURPHY

So, what do you do if you've been made to wait and wait and wait and then been told that the meeting will have to be postponed? Bite your tongue and roll with it or you will have allowed Murphy to end whatever relationship you could have had with this new client.

I assume that this was an important client. Don't let your emotions lose that client. Never show your frustration in an obvious way. Never upset a client (or a client's assistant—assistants tell on you!). Can you imagine the confusion on the part of your new client who doesn't even know you when her assistant says that you were upset and stormed out of the office? If I were your new client, it would be toodle-oo for you.

Still, you need to acknowledge the inappropriate behavior when you finally do meet or call. Notice that I said when *you call*. Take charge. Ask the assistant, "Is everything okay? Was there an emergency?" (Do this without a hint of sarcasm, it might really be an emergency.) Often an assistant will give you a little hint as to what occurred. Ask the assistant when the client will be free today or tomorrow or, if necessary, for the balance of the week. Then say, "I'll call tomorrow morning to reschedule. How's that time frame?" The assistant will often help make this happen to help cover the boss's indiscretion of breaking the meeting at the last minute.

Finally, remember to relax. To paraphrase a popular adage, things happen. Give the client the benefit of the doubt. Maybe next time it will be you that needs that benefit.

BOTTOM LINE

Don't take a late or canceled meeting personally. Let the client know that you noticed the delay or cancellation, but then move on positively. Keep your concentration on the important goal: Make that sale!

CHAPTER

7

MURPHY'S LAW
ON CLIENTS

EACH ONE IS LIKE AN ICEBERG—
WHAT YOU NEED TO KNOW IS
BELOW THE SURFACE

A few years ago I was in Chicago to coach a client in advertising sales on increasing the effectiveness of her selling techniques. Bright, eager, and polished, she seemed considerably talented, an astute salesperson with strong communication skills. But, in this case, her formidable communication skills were the problem: too good by half.

At the start of our morning together we met for coffee and discussed what she expected from that day's sales calls. She laid out a reasonable set of goals and showed levelheaded confidence in her ability to articulate what she would offer her clients. *Indeed, in each client visit that day she laid out a succinct, compelling pitch that emphasized the value of advertising in her magazine.*

Unfortunately, her style of sales call also included leading clients to say pretty much just what she wanted to hear. "It looks as though your target will still be men 18 to 35, right?" she'd ask. The client would immediately nod, "yes." "And your advertising season will be concentrated in the fall?" she'd continue. "As a matter of fact," the client would answer, "yes." Pleased with the "success" of her questions, she proceeded along these lines with each client. That's how it went for the entire meeting, every meeting.

She made no mistakes and was fully knowledgeable—the coast looked clear of Murphy, but it turned out that he was in such plain sight she couldn't see him.

At the end of the day we met for dinner and debriefing. I sincerely praised her clear understanding of each advertiser with whom we had met, but I had to ask her why we bothered to meet with anyone in the first place. "After all," I said, "we certainly didn't need to, since there wasn't a single question you asked that you didn't also answer. All day today you played both salesperson and client." There was a long pause as my coaching got through.

It's one thing to showcase your understanding of your client's situation in your opening comments. It's another to lead the witness, only to end up with what your research told you versus what the real deal is from your clients, the insights only they can provide. Even if you know the specific answer to your question, clients have information that you do not know, information that you need. The point of asking questions is to allow your clients to reveal themselves through their answers. Ask clients probing questions. Let them answer.

LISTEN AND GROW RICH

MURPHY STRIKES

Sometimes (too often, in fact) I get clients who seem to answer every question with a simple yes, no, or some other staccato reply that leaves me doing all the talking. I didn't go into this business to be a dentist, so why am I spending so much time pulling teeth?

In the title of his fine, insightful book, Napoleon Hill recommends that you "think and grow rich." Inspired by that message, I've tailored it to meet what I see is the single most important key to successful sales: Listen and grow rich. It doesn't matter how much you may know (or think you know), how uninteresting your client may be, or how brilliant and thorough your preparation has been, you will only benefit by listening to what your client has to say.

What usually passes for listening is anything but. We say we listen to the morning news while we get ready for the day even though our attention is divided between the electric toothbrush, the coffee maker, and clatter of the household as we scurry about performing our routines. We ask how people are and call it listening even though, before receiving a reply, in our mind we've already heard an answer of "fine"—it lets us move on with the conversation without the bothersome detail of having to actually wait for a response.

This is not listening. Listening is not what happens when your mind is simply occupied by sound. It is not going through the motions of maintaining a reasonable amount of silence after asking someone a question. It is not a knee-jerk knowing nod when it appears a sign of agreement is called for. It is not a respectful chuckle when you hear a joke you don't get.

Listening is opening your mind to what someone is saying, letting that information in, and then understanding it. When you meet with your client, you must be ready to absorb what is said, think about it, and process it. It is the essence of your relationship with the client. It is the only way you can meet the client's needs. Listening is at the heart of fulfilling your obligations as a salesperson. Without it, there is no success.

STEVE BUSTS MURPHY

So what about our tooth-pulling interviewer? You're determined to be an astute listener, but all you get are responses of yes, no, and maybe.

Design your questions, in advance, so that they can *only* be answered with an explanation instead of just a yes or no. Don't ask, "Are you expecting an increase in revenues next year?" Instead try, "What do you think of next year's projected revenues?" When clients aren't forthcoming with data, ask their opinion. Nine times out of ten, they have an opinion, and opinions are essential to understanding your client's point of view beyond the "party line" or tight-fisted information you may be getting.

BOTTOM LINE

The purpose of listening is to gather more than data. Ask open-ended questions. Seek explanations and opinions.

MAKE THE INTERVIEW GREAT

MURPHY STRIKES

The other day, my client gave a 20-minute, blow-by-blow recap of her 6-year-old's performance in a church play. Attempts to bring her back to business were fruitless until the whole story was told, and believe me this was *not* the greatest story ever told. I could barely maintain consciousness, let alone interest. How could I have gotten back on track?

It's not an IRS audit, folks. Sales interviews should be relaxed, thorough, natural—this is about establishing an ebb and flow. As you probe, you discover, which naturally leads you to ask the right questions. A sales call is unlike any other interview. It must be a relaxed conversation between two people. Two people who care about the same issue and share common goals.

Often, however, you need to care more than your clients about the issues at hand for them to begin caring about you. When you first meet clients, they frequently are not in the market for what you're selling. Your research has shown that there is a genuine need for your product or services, *but your clients may not see it yet.* Relax. If you nuance the interview correctly, you will establish an atmosphere of trust and aspiration. This atmosphere will allow them to explain their business goals and naturally allow them to understand where your product or service may perfectly fit in.

Great sales interviews flow naturally. Laughter, humanity, and genuineness are qualities that make all relationships real, including a sales call. These qualities increase trust, and when the sales interview is over, clients find themselves in a different place from where they started. Great sales interviews *change things*. They change how you are viewed. They change how your product is viewed. They confirm that you can do what you say you can do.

In a great sales interview the salesperson conveys, "I'm in this thing as much as you, if not more because my reputation as a salesperson is on the line. If I don't help you, I don't have a sale. Without that sale, I don't have a business."

So, you ask, how is it done? It's a lot easier than you think. First, understand that the primary goal of a meeting is a conversation. Its first priority is *not* collecting data or building a convincing case for your service or product. These are secondary goals.

People know when you're there for the money, and they know when you're there for the humanity. You can't hide it. You must want to appreciate what your client says. You must do your best to relate to it. Then you must let your client know you understand.

Under no circumstances should you allow your opinions to interfere with what your clients are trying to communicate. Do not dismiss their comments. Do not rush them. Do not lead them. Clients know when you're giving them short shrift. It's the number one sales killer.

Practice might make perfect, but it also makes permanent. Practice your ability to listen. Force yourself to do it right. Hone this skill. Do it again and again until it's habit. It's the one habit that will make the largest and most positive contribution to your career.

STEVE BUSTS MURPHY

Okay, you've dedicated yourself to a lively, natural give-and-take, but your client goes off on some inane tangent about the kids, poodle, or last night's bingo game. So how can you get back on track?

Always establish a clear agenda at the start of the sales call. This gives you the *opportunity and permission* to monitor the progress of your meeting and shift gears as necessary to get the result you both agreed upon at the start of the meeting. That agenda was compromised by this tangent. When the client veers from the agenda, don't encourage the story with a "what happened then" response. Try a quiet smile that doesn't denigrate the story, but doesn't keep it going either. That said, however, under certain circumstances it's advisable to listen to the story. The client obviously has something she simply must share and when you listen, it communicates respect, understanding, and patience.

BOTTOM LINE

Stick to your agenda and make sure your client does too. But, no matter what, listen to whatever your client has to say.

THE SIX ESSENTIAL GUIDELINES FOR A SUCCESSFUL INTERVIEW

MURPHY STRIKES

I've got a great product that I really love to share with clients, and if a client has a problem, I'm really good at solving it. I deliver. But, I've got to admit that I'm hardly the wittiest or most animated speaker. I've never been able to tell a joke, so I don't even try, and I find small talk downright irritating. A lot of clients appreciate my no-nonsense approach, but it leaves others cold. I love the nuts and bolts of sales, I just can't stand the pointless chitchat. Am I doomed?

Successful interviews combine myriad elements of style, nuance, and skill, but the critical requirements can be boiled down to six essential guidelines:

1. Be genuinely interested in the client.

2. Have your questions written out like a carpenter's punch list.

3. Let clients answer questions on their own. Don't lead the witness.

4. Be flexible. Know when to drill down. Know when to move on.

5. Make it fun.

6. Discover your client's frustration or problem and fix it.

Be genuinely interested in the client.

Dale Carnegie once said that after meeting someone he always knew more about the person than the person would know about him. It wasn't that he had anything to hide; he was genuinely interested in the other person and learning from them. As Emerson put it, "Every man I meet is my superior in some way. In that, I learn from him."

We live in a time of intense jadedness and skepticism. "Unless you 'wow' me, ASAP, I don't need what you're selling." This pressure leads people to resort to blasting into a sales call or meeting with a "bang" of an idea, or "breakthrough" concept that is pure genius, or so they hope. They dramatically espouse the virtues of their blessed idea, product, or service with adjectives and phrases normally reserved for comic books. The problem is that *none of this hyperbole takes the client's needs into consideration.* You might think that if you and I were talking together now I would be raising my voice. You are correct.

You must first listen to clients before you can address their needs. It sounds simple, but it's amazing how few salespeople follow this rule. In my direct observations of thousands of salespeople, few of them know how to listen. It's a lesson that even I continue to learn.

I have a great client in Canada who ranks, in all my years of coaching salespeople, as one of the finest sales professionals I've ever known, a man with profound sales instincts. One day while I was helping him with a new presentation, he began discussing his sales staff, specifically detailing their poor selling skills. Once he got started, I had to bite my tongue. I kept thinking, "What are you talking about? You're their boss so you're the one responsible for just how stinking they are! Check the mirror, pal!"

But, I didn't say anything. Instead, I just listened—for 30 minutes. During this half hour I noticed my feelings move from anger to empathy. As he talked, he revealed his frustration with himself as a coach and mentor, giving little blame to his staff. Without me saying anything, he ended his complaint with a very genuine request for help in becoming a better leader for these salespeople. If I had confronted him rather than listened, I would have teed him off and completely missed an opportunity to take specific actions to change his management style from critique-machine to player-coach.

Have your questions written out like a carpenter's punch list.

Remember the director of operations from the luxury retailer that I spoke of in the Introduction, the one who appreciated that I needed information from her before I could offer my services? Having a list of questions—even the ones scribbled on a scrap of paper in the taxi as I was headed to her office, gave me the basic information I needed to discover this client's needs. This is a perfect example of the importance of writing down questions before a sales meeting. A carpenter's punch list is a list of unfinished matters that *require* attention. Similarly, your list should itemize all issues (things you *must* know about before you can proceed) that require your attention.

Let clients answer questions on their own. Don't lead the witness.

It's one thing to showcase your understanding of your client's situation in your opening comments. It's another thing entirely to lead the witness, ending up with only the information that you already obtained from your research versus what's the real deal from the client. Your advance reconnaissance and all the details it gave are only part of the issue. Just like the salesperson from Chicago learned, you are not having a meeting to confirm how great your information is; you are there to gather information—particularly the client's view of the facts.

Be flexible. Know when to drill down.
Know when to move on.

A cardinal rule of selling is to be flexible. When initiating a sales dialogue with a prospective client or current client, you must understand the importance of listening. It tells you more than just facts; it gives you insight into the hidden needs and wants of the client—that iceberg below the surface.

There are times when a client will utter a seemingly innocuous word or phrase that is critical to your sale. Your job is to pick up that innocuous phrase and turn it into a specific gap in the needs and wants of your client. When you hear these words they should *sound an alarm.*

Watch for the following:

Always. "We always lighten up inventory in August."
A team of people involved with the same issue. "I'll be interested in Todd and William's ideas on applying your plan." (This, by the way, would be your cue to ask to be in on the meeting when Todd and William hear your idea, rather than having it filtered through a third party.)
Bad. "Everybody who went with the new product did great, and it made the rest of us look bad."

Frustration. "Sometimes the frustration level around here is through the roof."

Gap. "We're seeing a gap between our customers and our line."

Main issue. "The main issue is our customers, turnaround, and next quarter's returns."

Mandate or mission. "Our mandate is to increase customer satisfaction, regardless of costs."

Must. "You must have seen the article about us in the *Wall Street Journal.*"

Risk. "We took a risk last season and we got burned."

The boss's name. "What Ms. Harris expects is on-time delivery."

Vital. "On-time delivery is vital."

Worry. "My worry is that our sales team may not generate the volume we need for this quarter."

These are just some of the possibilities. Understand that your client will rarely come out and blatantly state, "I have a problem." Again, look below the surface and know when to drill down.

Probing means looking for that match between you and the client. This begins with being flexible enough to digress from your well-engineered probing list of questions and create, instantaneously, a series of questions that focus on the exact point that your client has just touched on that your instinct or intuition determines is significant. In other words, when you see the match, recognize it and drill down.

Imagine you're with a client and you are asking your established probing questions. She's just communicated how her stores maintain customer loyalty when she says, "That's our loyalty campaign, but that doesn't help gain new customers." Instantly you need to say to yourself, "Whoa! This might be an area, which I didn't identify during my research, where I can be of help." Shift gears quickly and naturally. If you genuinely care about the person and company that you are interviewing, you will be quite natural in your spontaneity and ready to ask these types of drill-down questions:

1. Whom do you need to attract?

2. By when do you need to attract them?

3. What medium will you use?

4. What amount will you dedicate to this effort?

Knowing when to move on is a little trickier. Does the client look away or become distracted? He may use the phrase, ". . . and that's all I know." He may change the subject and begin to get excited about a different topic. These are signs that you need to begin probing with open-ended questions to understand what the excitement is all about. Home in on that excitement and fit your sales call to meet it.

Make it fun.

Interviews need to be light and conversational. It's important to stick to the agenda, but make room for people to unwind when they go off on a tangent. Laugh with them when they say something that truly is funny to you. Listen carefully to whatever they say—complaints, family business, their interests—it will tell you something about them. It will also begin to relax them and, in turn, you. It will give you an opportunity to relate to their thoughts and offer your own related thoughts, thus sharing a part of yourself. The result is a closer relationship, better communication, and improved opportunity for sales.

Fun, however, doesn't mean less than serious. Your interview must follow a natural, logical flow, but must be based on solid research.

As you did your research, a puzzle began untangling. You started to see exactly where your product or service fits in. In the interview process, craft your questions to help reveal the mystery that your earlier research has uncovered. This means your questions will follow a natural progression. You will, of course, ask a certain number of questions to confirm your research. Then, build on these basic questions. Amplify your research. Expand it. Learn.

Discover your client's frustration or problem and fix it.

I was once in Hong Kong (a city where business is the only game in town) interviewing Frank, the division president of American Express, on the strengths of his sales force, which stretched from southern Asia to Australia. He began by reviewing his observations made since he had taken over his division the previous spring. He told me his disappointment in his salespeople and managers for not communicating a consistent corporate message to their clients throughout his region, giving several specific examples. After hearing his litany on what appeared to be a clear pattern, I asked him what the downside of this inconsistency was.

Talk about pushing the right button! Frank bristled as he explained how because of the lack of a consistent, clear value story and corporate message, the ability to generate increased sales would be significantly hampered. Sales would not be firm; they would be temporary, thus sabotaging his sales targets and the results he had to deliver to his superiors within the year.

It doesn't always hit you that hard, but as Frank unfolded his story, he revealed a significant frustration, one that he, literally, woke up to every morning and went to sleep with every night. By letting Frank vent and thoroughly explain the issue, I was then able to see how I could help his team. In my mind I began to create a critical path for my recommendations to him, ways that would let him get a handle on a situation that, for him, was quite unwieldy. But the only way I was able to get to this point was with patience. *Allow your client the time to fully explain the issue.*

Frank's word selection—the invocation of his boss's name, for example—underscored his frustration. My ability to empathize set the foundation for us to bond. I began my sales presentation with his exact phrases and confirmed with him that these were his specific frustrations. This put him a little more at ease and allowed me to then begin to explain how I would solve his problems.

Remember, you don't really sell anything. You are there to make things better, repair damage, solve a problem. You fix things. You've done the research, and you know that you have something that's good for the client. Your job is to let your client understand that you are the one who can make things better through sophisticated questioning, careful listening, and thoughtful responses. Present yourself as an astute professional, an expert who can solve problems, someone they can trust to fix what's wrong.

Once you let clients talk it out, you can fully understand their problems. And solving those problems is why you're there.

Next, prioritize your questions from your client's point of view. Determine what question needs to be asked first, then second, then third, and so on until you have completed the list of questions that need to be resolved to determine if your product or service is a match.

Probing accomplishes four fundamental steps to selling:

1. Fact-finding

2. Driving a spontaneous inquiry

3. Acknowledging a frustration

4. Pinpointing an opportunity

When you first begin your probing, you are naturally fact-finding and confirming your research. As the questions progress, you drive a spontaneous inquiry that culminates in an acknowledged frustration on the part of your client, which leads you to the opportunity for your product to come to the rescue to alleviate the frustration. Here are two examples of probing questions that start out fact-finding and then lead to a specific inquiry.

Consider an advertising salesperson meeting with a health-food bar maker. The salesperson must convince the manufacturer that the magazine is an appropriate advertising vehicle. The questions might progress in this way:

1. From my research I see that your target age for advertising your health bar is 18 to 24 years. Besides the age, how would you describe the typical person in this age group?

2. How do you plan on expanding your market?

3. Which markets represent your strongest growth?

4. Which companies make up your competitive set this year?

5. Describe your creative advertisement for this year.

6. What barriers do you see for reaching the demographic that we've just discussed?

I now know the target audience, the desired client, the marketing (advertising) thrust, and a problem that I am able to solve.

Here's another example. My client is looking for increased traffic and sales at her department store. I ask:

1. Who do you most want to attract this season?

2. What amount will you be investing to accomplish this?

3. When will you begin the process?

4. What media will you employ to do this?

5. What is your largest concern regarding the success of this project?

Again, I now have goals, a marketing thrust, a schedule, and a problem ready for me to solve.

By prioritizing your questions *you establish a logical progression in your client's mind that naturally leads to the product or service you offer*. Now you are ready to sell.

An effective interview begins with a solid base of preparation. It's all about being ready for the interview with the right questions in the right order, dramatically impressing the client with your interviewing skills after your second question. ("Wow, this guy really gets it!") It will happen if you do your homework.

STEVE BUSTS MURPHY

Okay, we've established that the interview must follow a natural give-and-take, but you're convinced that your aversion to chitchat condemns you to less than stellar sales meetings. You're not doomed. Just substitute pointless chitchat with tailored chitchat. Human beings are social animals. We require insight into the people we are transacting business with to see and understand their personalities. Understanding personalities allows us to get closer, to establish trust.

Remember people buy people first and product second. By crafting tailored chitchat, you remain true to your no-nonsense approach, but also let an important part of you come to the surface. Select your opening comments specifically with your client in mind. This way even the most businesslike approach won't leave the client cold. Speak to clients in terms that they can relate to, terms that are part of their business. A perfect example of tailored chitchat is news that affects their industry. You can pick up this news from major newspapers or business journals or online. Reading the top stories about their industry gives you depth of knowledge and a chance to be client-focused, sophisticated, and by definition no-nonsense with your chitchat.

BOTTOM LINE
Be yourself. If pointless small talk puts you off, then make your small talk have a point.

THE SEVEN SECRET WANTS

MURPHY STRIKES
I'm there for my clients and like to help out in any way that I can. But, I got great Knicks tickets for one client as a thank you for a large sale, and ever since she hasn't been shy about asking for them again and again. It turns out that she uses them as a bragging point with her colleagues, a fairly hard-core sports bunch. I not only hate having to scramble to try to get them (and often failing), I also feel a bit used. Am I stuck as her own personal Ticketron? And please don't tell me to just put my foot down; that sale was far too big for me to not answer her calls.

When you meet a client, of course you want to know about the coming season and the issues facing the client's company, but what you're really searching for here is what the critical need of that individual is within the company. You need to determine the metric of your client's success and understand how the client is judged in the company, what will make a difference in getting a raise, and what will determine the size of the year-end bonus. People will tell you the metric of their success, but you have to ask. It is here where you get to know their "secret" wants.

In fact, the easiest way to know you've done it right is when you've got somebody lamenting about her problem. If you are able to help her, then you've got the sale.

Everybody, from the school crossing guard to the CEO in the cushiest office, has secret wants. These wants motivate and inspire. Sometimes they cause fear. Your job is to discover your client's wants, understand them, and respond to them. Though they take many forms, most of the secret wants of your clients fall under one of seven simple categories.

1. People want to look good—to their superiors, their colleagues, themselves, and to you.

2. They want someone to ease their burden.

3. They want to avoid embarrassment.

4. They want their problems solved.

5. They want their work with you to be painless.

6. They want good results.

7. They want to save time.

People want to look good.

Image isn't everything, but it's a lot. You contribute to your clients' image through recommendations that will make them look good. This is an important part of your responsibility as a salesperson. This needs to show in your sales interviews. Clients need to feel that you care about their image and understand that preserving and enhancing that image is as important as your actual recommendation.

If, for example, a client asks you to deliver a presentation to his team in order to resolve the team's questions about your product, it's also a request to present that client in a good light to the sales team—the client, after all, is the one who got you there. Show you understand the importance to your client's prestige and image by asking critical questions, such as:

Who will be at the meeting?

How are they connected to the client?

Who will be in charge at the meeting?

Who needs to be impressed?

Is anybody in the group particularly negative or hard to please?

Who are your champions?

How does the team usually make a decision?

What is your expectation of how the meeting ought to end in order to further the sale?

People want someone to ease their burden.
Most of your clients have significant burdens. They face pressure to deliver favorable results to their customers, company's shareholders, and to their immediate superiors. A master salesperson pinpoints these burdens and eases the client's burden with a

product or service. Once you discover this burden, you know at least one critical need, and this presents you with an opportunity to fulfill that need.

People want to avoid embarrassment.

Each salesperson and every sales consultant is an extension of the client. You perform a role that is critical to the client's success. The client is, in essence, your constituent. Clients are your responsibility, and so you have the responsibility to support them, guide them, serve them, and meet their needs by meeting your obligations, just as an elected official must meet the needs of the voters.

This support means keeping clients informed on any issue and any situation that may need their attention—giving them a "heads up." Too often salespeople get distracted with other clients or new sales, but if you can't keep track of your original client, what's the point of moving on to others? It's a bit of self-flattery (and fun) to think of ourselves as selling machines, grinding out sales to achieve our sales goals. But, you're only as good as your last performance, the last good thing you did for a client.

To that end, you must keep impeccable records and an impeccable calendar. You must know how your client fits into those records and calendar and be able to make her aware *before* something with the potential to backfire does. Know when to go back to a client with a progress report detailing what has occurred that has helped his business and avoided possible pitfalls.

You are the eyes and ears in this business relationship. When I noticed one client's sales team working on autopilot in their presentations, it was up to me to pass this information along to my client. Other times I've seen salespeople who just shouldn't be selling, and it was my job to explain to the vice president of sales explaining that this person was miscast and hurting the business. Sometimes your recommendation may be offering services, in addition to the ones you originally set out to bring them, that will aid their overall business.

These sorts of advance warnings avoid ill feelings and embarrassing situations for you and the client and keep you in the role as problem solver. Keep in mind that once a client has been hurt, it can take months or years to regain her trust and confidence. Be aware and ready to act to prevent troubles.

People want their problems solved.

Clients don't see you because they want to make another friend. They see you because they have a hunch that there is something that you can fix or improve, something that can help them achieve their goal of improvement. They are dealing with something that needs to be rectified. Your job is to find it. Think of it as a hidden treasure. It is the treasure of a successful sales call.

Once you discover the problem, you need to solve it or at least contribute to its resolution. Your reputation depends on it. Your company's reputation and its product or service depends on it. And, finally, your relationship with your client depends on it.

People want their work with you to be painless.

People don't need a headache. This means that you need to avoid causing hassles in any way, shape, or form. You must navigate through the selling process in ways that minimize the steps your client needs to take. Your clients have enough work to do without you and your product or service adding more. Anytime you need to ask your clients to deliver something or resolve an issue, your request gets added to their other duties. Any requests must be presented in such a way that your client can self-realize the importance of addressing the requests in a timely manner.

People want good results.

Of course, clients want good results. So do you. It's essential to have a metric, a measurement, attached to your product or service in order to present the success of your efforts. By going with your product, the client can expect improvement as a result. It will be quantifiable. In fact, you two must agree on the exact measurement or metric of what will qualify as a "success" of your product. Will it be more customers, increased sales, or expanded market reach? Set the measurement and meet it. It's important to have the measurement completed and ready to share before clients have to do it themselves.

Note: Be very careful what metric you assign to your product because you will have to meet it. Make sure that it is reasonable and fair to all involved, including you.

People want to save time.

Time is precious. Time is money. Time waits for no one.

There's a good reason for the countless adages about not wasting time: As Ben Franklin said, "It's the stuff life's made of." Your duty as a salesperson is to offer things to the client that are always turnkey—ideas, services, products, plans that put the key in the ignition and get things going.

Clients want to feel that you are in control and have a specific time line as to when and what results will be produced. This lets them get back to their other responsibilities. Frank, my American Express client in Hong Kong, needed a 1-year plan that would standardize the sales-client interactions of his Asia team. My job was to manage Frank's expectations by meeting with him at specific points in the year to debrief him on the results that were produced to date and the next steps of his training program that were going to be delivered. Because I had a clear system to present to Frank he had no reason to worry that he needed to be any more involved in the process than what he was.

In turn, Frank saw me as an ally that he did not have to shadow to ensure good results. Frank faced many difficulties that year that kept him occupied, but not one moment of those 12 months was wasted by me.

STEVE BUSTS MURPHY

But what should you do about the client who makes no secret of her desire to be the person in her office who can score the best basketball seats to the hottest games? You're not stuck being her personal Ticketron as long as you expand your business relationship with her. There is always a next step to any business transaction, including a thank-you gift. Your next step is to make the next sale. If you're not sure of the next sale, arrange a probing meeting to understand how the sale that you did make helped her.

As you collect this feedback begin thinking about other products or services that could further your indispensable nature to her. These actions show her that people get Knicks tickets when they are continual customers of yours, not just one-timers. As the meetings progress and you expand your business relationship with her, slow down or stop the Knicks tickets. Coupling these two actions will show her that transacting business, not perks, is at the heart of your work with her.

Besides, expanding your relationship from just one big sale to a series of sales that bring her closer to her business goals this year will impress her colleagues a lot more than a detailed description of Latrell Spreewell's sweaty jump shot.

BOTTOM LINE

Just as in any other case where the client loses focus of the important issues at hand, make concerted efforts to redirect the interest from the fun of the perks to the benefits of your product.

IS YOUR HUNCH CORRECT?

MURPHY STRIKES

I thought I had a pretty good handle on my new client, but my ideas were totally off the mark. What I took to be an expanding operation in Europe was being scaled back. The American market focus was being shifted to an older clientele, a total departure from their traditional stance. In other words, even though I did my homework, the client meeting was one revelation after another. It was hard for

me to keep my footing, and I think it showed. Should I
have just come out and said I was surprised or acted like
I was in the know all along?

You go into a sales meeting with some idea of what's up with
each client, but is your hunch right? Each customer is different,
with individual dreams and expectations. Each business is different, with individual problems and assets. Your interview is
to get a fix on the individual so that you can tailor your solution to fit that exact situation.

The interview is your opportunity to be sure about what you
should already have a pretty good handle on. It's not a fishing
trip. You're not trolling just to see what bites. The last thing you
want is an answer that totally takes you by surprise.

So, Bob, what are you looking for in men's athletic
apparel sales next year?

We sold our athletic line in August.

And whatever you do, don't be caught using a lousy probing
question. Listed here are the 10 worst probing questions and
why they should be avoided.

The 10 Worst Probing Questions

1. *How's business?* You should know how business is. At the
   very least you should have a general understanding of the
   trends in that particular industry. Even if you haven't studied
   the segment of business extensively, you want to know enough
   to get through a conversation about your client's industry.

2. *What are your goals for this year?* This should be part of your understanding of the client's business goals from your research, including online sources you've used to study the company. Also you should have talked with one or two lower-level executives to understand the business goals of the executive you are seeing.

3. *Who is your competition?* You must have this knowledge before your interview. It's basic. There are many ways to collect this data. Call someone at the company—even an administrative assistant will have a good understanding of the company's competitive set. Do online research with companies you believe are competitors. See who's doing what on the business page. Spend a buck and get the newspaper.

4. *What makes your product good?* Again, this is a basic homework chore for you. Try the product. If it's a restaurant, eat there. If it's a shoe store, buy a pair or at least try a pair on. Read about it. Study the company's Web site. Ask friends and business colleagues about the product. Ask a client who is a direct competitor (but keep it on the downlow, no need for jealousy).

5. *Has your product been successful in the past?* You need to know this ahead of time. It is, after all, history. Do the research. If you can't find out on your own, ask people who are familiar with the company about the firm's products and how successful they have been in the past.

6. *Who is your customer?* You should know. Study the company's Web site, ask people, ask employees of the company. Go to the store and see who's shopping there. Are they wear-

ing Ferragamos or flip-flops? What's the advertising posture? Who's on the product's label? If it's an older woman with gray hair, you can bet they're not aiming for the skateboarding set.

7. *Is there anyone else in the company I need to see?* There's almost always someone else to see. The question is, "Who else would be appropriate for me to meet with to determine their opinion as we move forward together?"

8. *Would you like this information that I prepared for you?* If you prepared information for someone, you had to have a strong belief that it was useful. Present the information as a gift. Hesitation communicates tentativeness. Only hold back on prepared information if you determined from your conversation it is inappropriate or has incorrect or old data.

9. *Do you have a sense of the problems your company faces this year?* Believe me, they do. The question is, "What frustrations have surfaced this year that must be addressed going forward?"

10. *What should I do next?* You need to determine from your meeting what your next step ought to be. You may not always be correct, but voicing the next step as an idea that you want your client to comment on or agree with is smart. Try saying, "Based on what we've discussed, it looks as though my next step is to meet with your acquisition team and determine its specific needs. Then we should meet to finalize our next step together. How does that sound?" Most clients enjoy being with someone who can take the proverbial ball and run with it. It shows activity and enthusiasm. And, if you are incorrect, they will let you know. They will

probably set up what your next step needs to be very clearly. The point of this is that when you initially leave it up to them without voicing your idea of what the next step should be, they often will procrastinate. Better to offer them the critical path you have just determined as a motivator that will either lead them to agree with your next action or offer one of their own. Either way, you win, because your meeting moves forward!

STEVE BUSTS MURPHY

Okay, so not only is your hunch not correct, you aren't even in the right ballpark. Strange things sometimes occur with clients, including coming up with a bunch of bad data from your reconnaissance. When your reconnaissance fails you, drop it and just listen. Immediately turn your presentation or selling meeting into a probing meeting. This is paramount because your own reputation is at stake. You cannot position yourself as someone with incorrect knowledge and hope to make a sale. At this point you can only listen to your client, probe him with open-ended questions to determine where he needs help, and retreat to live to sell again tomorrow.

BOTTOM LINE

When your research has sent you in the wrong direction of questions, immediately regroup. Assume no false posture of knowledge. Use the meeting to give you the information the reconnaissance failed to deliver.

8

THE BIG SHOW

PRESENTATIONS THAT EVIDENCE EXCELLENCE AND MUTE MURPHY

One of the small joys of being a man is the fact that we don't have to carry purses or, more to the point, we don't have to buy them. While I can appreciate a well-made, beautiful bag, it never fails to amaze me how much one of these items cost. But, it's a huge part of the women's apparel market, and when one upscale bag and luggage maker based in New York called me for help, I knew I would be working to help solve a big-ticket problem.

I assumed that I'd be asked to help the sales staff increase sales, but sales were actually quite good. What happened after the sale was the problem.

Specifically, the retailer told me, in the days and weeks following a sale, an inordinate amount of the product was being returned. The retailer had a sterling reputation. The bags were top quality, exquisitely detailed, and the height of fashion—so where, why, and how was Murphy sticking his finger into the mix?

To get to the bottom of it, I began by observing the sales staff. As befits this sort of high-end operation, they were well-groomed, articulate, and eager sellers. But, as my observations eventually revealed, eagerness was at the root of what was going wrong.

When customers came in, all the salespeople saw were dollar signs, not the needs of the customer. When a woman was looking for a bag, they'd determine her budget and then set about to convince her to get a bag for that budget—quick in, quick out, and another commission under the belt.

Too often, though, the ladies would discover that the bag they'd purchased wasn't right for their needs. Those who did a lot of business travel needed a bag that held a lot in several compartments. Those who took mass transit needed a bag with strong zippers or clasps. Each had needs. The sales staff ignored those needs. The result, in the long run, was failed sales.

The foundation of any successful sales presentation is knowing that what you offer the client fulfills the needs of the client. The client must be clear on what you have to offer and why. After you've heard your client's needs from the interview part of the meeting, you can then make a presentation that works. As the staff of that luggage retailer found out, you earn a lot more money from a satisfied customer than from a returned tote.

Hallelujah, it's time to sing!

You've read, you've researched, you've practiced, you've probed. You did everything you were supposed to do. Now, it's show time. The piano has played the introduction, and you're ready to hit that first note, ready to kill, wow, and scintillate.

Whoa, Nellie!

Before you go on, you must consider all the reasons why presentations—your audition before the client—fail. Why do some presentations fly with excitement and others turn out as dry as a sidewalk in the Sahara? What makes a presentation drift irreparably off the mark, leaving an unfocused message that hints of real arrogance on the part of the salesperson?

Herb Greenberg, Harold Weinstein, and Patrick Sweeney's book, *How to Hire and Develop Your Next Top Performer*, sums up the essential characteristic or quality of successful selling in one word, empathy. According to the authors, "only with sufficient empathy to recognize the real needs of a prospect can those needs be met through the product or services being sold." Empathy is the holy grail of selling.

So, master empathy and all is solved? Not quite, but all great sales presentations require empathy evidenced by a salesperson who clearly demonstrates that the client's needs and wishes will be met through their recommendation.

With that as your basis, you are now ready to concentrate on how you present that message.

BODY LANGUAGE NEVER STOPS TALKING, SO WATCH WHAT YOU SAY

MURPHY STRIKES

I was in the middle of a critical point in the presentation, and my client started toying with his watch, lost in thought. I was talking about issues of critical importance to his company and he seemed to care less. Besides shaking him very gently by the throat, what could I do?

A huge amount of communication is physical delivery. Humans respond to gestures and movements like any other animal. When you approach a dog, for example, do you think it cares whether or not you're saying "good boy"? No, it looks at your movements, your tone, and your physical stance as you get closer. We're not dogs, of course, but we react essentially in the same way. If movement and tone are friendly, we react with openness and interest. Stiffness, reticence, and timidity result in reluctance, wariness, and concern.

Consider the formidable communication skills of Bill Clinton or Tony Blair. We're not talking politics, we're talking style, and these two have it in spades. These are men who grasp the podium, almost hug it as they embrace their task. When they offer a big point, they make a grand sweeping gesture. When they dive into minutia, they draw their fingers to a tight point, as though they were seizing their words in tweezer tips. And when they make a vow or promise, they clench their fists in a defiance that almost dares you to disagree.

A half century ago, it was Franklin D. Roosevelt who held center stage as he charmed and cajoled with a confident, compassionate tone in his voice that bespoke knowledge and strength. It was said that critics of the president refused to listen to his famous fireside chats on the radio, so beguiling was his presentation. Instead, they waited for a printed transcript so they could pick apart what he said without the distractions of who was saying it.

Several years ago, at the end of a long day, I had one more sales delivery to make. It was a Friday afternoon in the heat of a New York summer. (For those of you who have never had the joy of experiencing a steamy summer afternoon in the Big Apple, imagine taking a dip in a pan of hot dog water to get an idea of what it's like to trudge through this kind of oppressive weather.) On this particular day, despite the heat and humidity (turns out, by the way, it's not either one, it's both), I was determined to wring out a decent delivery for my final sales call.

As I was making my presentation, I noticed my client looking around, playing with his wedding ring, fidgeting, and generally disconnected from our conversation. We were ensconced in an air-conditioned office, but I wondered if the weather hadn't zapped his attention. Then, I began to think, "Oh, a wise guy, huh? Well, sorry, Charlie. I'm going to look right at you whether you return the eye contact or not and give you the finest, most impassioned presentation I can."

As I completed the presentation and closed him on the next step, which was to agree to a new training program, he looked at me and said, "Great! Let's do it!"

Dumbfounded, I said, "Excuse me, but throughout my presentation you didn't seem very interested." He replied, "I know, I was just testing you to see if you could hold my attention. You proved you could; now I want your program for my entire company."

It was the biggest sale I made that year, and it created a profound relationship with this individual. Turns out he was and is a masterful salesperson, one of the finest I know and someone who really appreciated my delivery style, the time I took to craft the presentation, and my perseverance in the face of his testing.

As a salesperson, of course, mastery of your physical delivery can only be rewarded if it's built on solid content. Once you have that, though, almost everything depends on how you bring it across.

THE SIX SUREFIRE WAYS TO FIRE IT UP

1. Look at me.

As John Travolta said countless times in the movie *Get Shorty*, "Look at me!" Okay, so maybe it wasn't an Oscar performance, but those three words effectively convey a core issue of communication, a simple rule that too many salespeople give short shrift, to their own disadvantage. *You must look at the client*.

Looking at a client while speaking is a must. It's such an easy thing to understand, yet it cannot be taken for granted. I've seen countless salespeople begin a conversation without looking at their client. I have seen salespeople break eye contact from a client in the middle of a sentence, as though concern for the client was being dropped midsentence, too. Some salespeople even go so far as to look away from the client when answering a question.

These actions communicate that you are preoccupied with something other than your client. While you're going on in your detached style, Murphy has sidled up to the client and pointed out how lack of eye contact usually means "Sorry, client, but I'm a little nervous here" or "Wait a minute, client, I just lost my place" or, worse, . . . "I just need one more second to fabricate an answer."

It sounds like such a no-brainer, but sometimes we don't use our brains! Looking at people is the most important physical delivery skill a salesperson has. Never forget it. Looking directly at someone says many things all at once. It communicates relationship. It says, "I care. You're important. This subject is important. And, not incidentally, I'm important too."

Eye contact regulates your warmth factor with a client. Too little of it and there is no warmth. A lot of it (and I'm not talking about burning a hole in somebody with the wide-eyed stare of a cult member) and you've got a sale or at least a connection with a client who will, nine times out of ten, tell you the precise issues you need to resolve to make the sale. She will do that because you have conditioned her to see you as a very committed, no-nonsense salesperson.

Finally, eye contact communicates that something is at stake and cannot be trivialized or postponed, namely, your client's situation and your desire to help him.

2. Get into it.

Clients won't get jazzed unless you are. You are the catalyst for excitement and involvement. Next to the importance of eye contact, gesturing and being physically involved in your presentation are the most important of nonverbal activities.

The more involved you are physically, the more involved your client will become and the less opportunity there is for Murphy to advertise your tentativeness. Certainly you need to be appropriate to your client and the situation. You're not there as Crazy Eddie, but enjoy your presentation. Your physical involvement translates as enthusiasm.

That said, remember to not point your finger at a client. It's a sign you feel superior. Similarly, don't "tent" your hands by tapping your fingertips together. It's body language for "I know more than you do" (plus you'll look like a pompous idiot).

3. Don't slouch.

Your mother told you the same thing a thousand times, so let me say it once: Don't slouch. Sit up straight and stand up straight. It's easy to slouch in a chair, especially when your client does. It's particularly easy when seated on the client's couch or swivel chair. Hey! The meeting's going well, you feel relaxed, so you assume a casual posture.

But, posture is ego. If you slouch, you look like a slouch. If you sit up and stand up correctly, you look correct. Good posture communicates courage and conviction.

Don't, of course, act like you have a yardstick taped to your spine. (You will look stiff, and you will look like a stiff.) But, do take the time to maintain a natural, solid, upright stance.

When you are standing and delivering a presentation, don't pace. It's not a track meet. Pacing makes people wonder if you're about to leave the room. And while it's good to have physical motion, you don't want to be doing so much that they watch you instead of listen to you. Stand still and keep your weight equally distributed on both legs, otherwise you'll lean, which looks lazy, or begin rocking, which is also distracting.

4. Lose the monotone.

I can't think of a situation where a monotone fits, with the possible exception of Ben Stein's over-the-top turn in *Ferris Bueller's Day Off* ("Bueller? . . . Bueller? . . . Bueller? . . ."). Avoid a monotone at all costs. Clients need to hear your voice modulate through a presentation. Practice your delivery either in front of the mirror or use a tape recorder or Dictaphone to hear your voice and its vocal variety. Holding a client's attention with your voice requires that you modulate it as you speak.

If you have difficulty punching it up in terms of tone, concentrate on selected words that you especially want to connect with clients. Use your clients' words from your probing meetings to feed back to them. Use those words or phrases in a purposely spirited way (you don't have to be as extreme as Paul Prudhomme, but imagine underscoring a point by saying, "I guar-an-*tee* it!"). Clients love to hear their own words being spoken back to them; it proves you heard them and retained their goals. But, they need to hear it with some pep.

5. Slow down.

From New York to Los Angeles, London to Kyoto, many salespeople talk too fast (and, think about it, has the term "fast talker" ever had a nice connotation?). The client doesn't know the content as well as you do. You need to pause between statements to let people understand you as you deliver your information.

Clients won't ask you to back up once they've missed a point. Instead they are more likely to forget the point, which may lead to an objection to your sale later in the meeting because the information was missed.

Pace yourself. Give your thoughts and ideas the time they deserve to be understood. You've put hours into formulating your recommendations. Give those recommendations the time needed to communicate them.

6. Kill the nonwords.

Most nonwords and nonphrases are spoken without the speaker being aware of it. They say nothing of substance and everything of distraction. They do little more than fill space with irritating noise. Eliminate the following words and phrases from your vocabulary and your presentations:

- Ah

- Um

- You know (Do they know? If so, you don't need to tell them; if they don't know, then "you know" is completely out of place.)

- Like (This one's strictly for valley girls.)

- If you will (What if they won't?)

- Basically (If it's so basic, why do you have to point it out?)

- At the end of the day (Cliché alert!)

- Actually (Are you comparing what you are saying to, say, fantasy?)

- Truthfully (Has everything up to now not been truthful?)

- Okay? K? M'k?

- Well now (This is beyond folksy.)

These utterances reveal hesitance and uncertainty. That, in turn, makes the client feel hesitant and uncertain about you and your recommendations. Sounds like Murphy's in the room! And please, skip tired words and phrases such as "paradigm," "think outside the box," and "run it up the flagpole." As one editor once remarked to his writers, "Go easy on the clichés. I eat them for breakfast, lunch, and dinner."

So that's what you don't say. But, don't forget what you should say. Particularly, you should know how to speak to your clients in the lingo of their industry. If you don't know the difference between "SKU" and "Ska" when you go into a record store, you're sunk. Learn your client's lexicon.

STEVE BUSTS MURPHY

If you're doing everything right in a presentation, it won't make much of a difference if the client's not paying attention. As soon as you noticed him playing with his watch, you needed to immediately reengage your client. Whatever point you've just made, or are making,

repeat it in the form of a question ("It's not just expanding markets that's your goal, am I right? You're looking to
expand into quality markets, right?"). Then ask your
client's opinion. "What are you thinking in terms of that?"
It brings your client back and gives you a chance to redirect his attention to the material you're presenting and
how it fits in with his goals.

BOTTOM LINE

Keep track of your client's attention. If it flags, your
chances for making a connection—the linchpin of
sales—fall accordingly.

HOW TO BELLY FLOP, MURPHY STYLE

MURPHY STRIKES

I had a great presentation, fully laid out on paper. As
a courtesy to the client, I gave him a copy of it. The next
thing you know, he jumps ahead to the last page of my
printout presentation to see the price tag. Was I wrong to
share the presentation?

I've heard every excuse in the world about why a presentation
failed, from the salesperson not having enough sleep the night
before to the moon being in the wrong phase. Regardless of
the excuse, though, it remains exactly that: an excuse. Most
presentation failures can be boiled down to eight simple
reasons.

EIGHT REASONS WHY PRESENTATIONS FAIL

1. No link between the client and your product.

Presentations fail when they are not linked to solving the exact needs of the client. Salespeople must present their product or service within the context of the articulated needs of the client. Make the link. Obsess with drawing a straight line from the client's needs to your recommendations. Like an attorney before a jury, you must prove beyond a reasonable doubt that your recommendation matches the client's stated needs.

Presentations without linkage are plain arrogant. You may be nice as pie, but if your presentation is canned, you deserve to have the client say no. If you think you deserve respect, then earn it. Start by concentrating on making a link—it takes away the selfishness and puts the client first.

One way to be sure that your information meets the needs of the client is to repeatedly, throughout your presentations, begin your sentences with the phrase, "What this means for your business is . . ." These words specifically link you to your client's needs.

2. Lack of flexibility.

Presentations fail when the salesperson doesn't have the flexibility to accommodate his message as the moment may require. Salespeople are often hell-bent on delivering their message to the exclusion of all other reality, no interruptions or tangents tolerated.

Imagine if you went to see your doctor and he ignored you as you voiced questions, concerns, or fears about your health.

You'd think he only sees patients as statistics, simply people he needs to get past during his day.

Again, you need to show empathy. The client has concerns: *Answer them.* You know you have to show empathy during the probing part of the meeting. Empathy does not stop when your presentation begins; it increases.

One reason some salespeople maintain a rigid outlook during the presentation is because they're overwhelmed by the task. They become so involved with the presentation that they block out the ability to be natural and let their empathy show. Clients may ask questions during a presentation or they may just sit back and listen. Either way, the one thing they are always doing is observing you, watching and sensing your humanity. As they gauge your data, they also gauge your human touch. They feel the atmosphere you are creating as you deliver your presentation. Are you approachable? Are you calm? Are you open to questions? Are you explaining what's needed in order for clients to self-realize the importance of your product to solve their problems?

When clients determine that you are on a mission to deliver your recommendation with or without them by your side, they remove themselves from whatever equation you may be constructing. They wait for you to finish and then politely say that they need to think about it.

You end up going back to your office, scratching your head and wondering if your presentation communicated or not. We could ask Murphy to answer that one, but I'm betting you won't like the answer.

You figured your presentation went fine because you delivered a compelling argument for your product, but your message has been outdone by your arrogance as you concentrate on your own significance instead of the client's.

3. *Content not prioritized.*

Murphy can be controlled and harnessed by you, provided you are flexible enough to prioritize the content of your presentation to the needs of the individual client. Rigidity results from poorly ordered facts within the presentation, important information not prioritized according to the prospect's goals and challenges. Incorrectly ordered facts communicates that the salesperson is more interested in selling product versus truly solving an expressed business problem.

Proper research before your first meeting will lead you to craft the correct open-ended probing questions needed to confirm that research and collect data from the client during your probing. Then you can tailor your presentation to mirror this information.

Keep yourself flexible so you can categorize your content from your prospect's frame of reference. Ideally, your content is in a seamless order. As you prepare your presentation, become the client. From that perspective, decide which statistic or fact goes where, which ones you need to communicate first and which can wait. It proves that you have not only heard their cry for help, but you will also deftly answer their plea.

Remember *Mission Impossible*? Think of Mr. Phelps, manager of the mission impossible team. Once the mission is assigned to him, his role (if he decides to accept it, of course) is to assemble the perfect team to succeed in accomplishing the mission. He carefully looks at dossiers and makes up his team.

When you design a presentation, assume the role of Mr. Phelps, assembling your data as though it was your team. Carefully select the data that you will use to accomplish each part of your mission in order of importance. Prove to clients that your product or service is precisely designed for their needs.

4. Too long.

When you select the data, don't overdo it. *More is not better.* Many presentations fail because they are too long.

I have listened to oodles of presentations that have too much data in them and end up confusing the prospect. Packing presentations with too much information (even though you swear that every piece of data is needed) takes the momentum out of your presentation and out of your prospect's desire to choose your product. Hi, Murphy! Back so soon?

Unfortunately it was you who opened the gate for Murphy to muck the presentation all up. He convinced you that more is better. Think about the best presentations you've ever given or seen given. What likely comes to mind is a feeling of natural momentum and rhythm, similar to the rhythm a great song has that stays with you throughout the day. The songwriter produces a great song by selecting only the notes needed to convey the song's message, no more no less, perfectly blending them to communicate the message.

Consider yourself like that songwriter. Your presentations should be music to your client's ears, with an intriguing, discernible rhythm to your message, accessible in its simplicity and clarity, one that stays with a client long after you've left.

5. No graphics to clarify the message.

Graphics simplify the message. The largest part of what we retain, we retain graphically. Think about it. When we recall something, we recall it in pictures not words. Yet many presentations have no supporting graphics to communicate the message.

As you make your presentation, graphically represent your message. You'll notice that it's easier for clients to recall your content if you show it in pictures beforehand.

As we've discussed earlier in this chapter, the client evaluates your delivery style as much as your message. Graphics give visual confirmation of your mastery of your presentation's content.

Here are three examples of clear graphics:

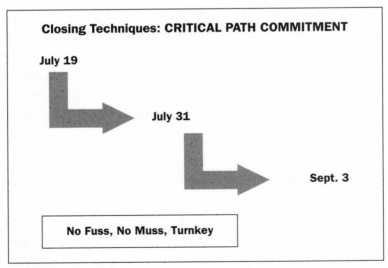

It's easier to communicate a series of next steps graphically versus in written form.

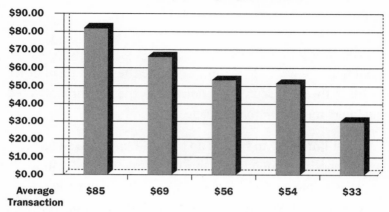

Using three-dimensional bar charts is clearer than just listing the data.

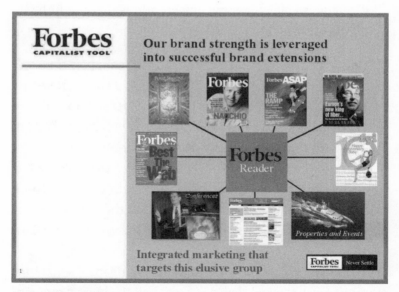

Rather than giving a write-up of each property, Forbes *magazine chose to graphically represent its stable of brand extensions this way.*

Without graphics, clients are much more likely to forget your message. Graphics are a road map that tells Murphy to get out of town.

6. Too many qualifiers.

Qualifiers are words that limit or dilute the meaning of other words in the same sentence. Look at how these commonly used qualifiers muddy up the message.

> What I'm going to try and do today, I hope, is to suggest that perhaps you choose our company to assist you in your company goals. If you see the value of our suggestions, what you might do is hire us to, hopefully, strengthen your goals. I want to make our discussion a dialogue, so please ask me any questions that might be on your mind.

How's that for pussyfooting around the main point?

Certainly there are times when qualifying your statements are necessary. But presentations, more often than not, are times for boldness. When I interviewed the publisher of one of the most widely read monthly magazines in America, I asked him for an assessment of the advertising salespeople he has worked with throughout his career. He didn't need to think twice. He pointedly explained that most of the time salespeople lack boldness, usually not putting forth their ideas in a confident way.

Tentative sales behavior automatically opens the gate for Murphy to waltz in and slow down and halt the buying momentum. Don't let this happen to you.

Compare the following statement to the tentative example above. Note the lack of qualifiers and the emphasis on direct communication.

What I'm going to do today is to recommend that you hire our company to reach your business goals. As you see the value of our recommendations, we are confident that you will hire us to strengthen those goals. It's important that our conversation be a dialogue, not a monologue, so please interrupt me whenever you have a question or concern.

Which example, the first or the second, would more likely draw your interest in the presentation about to be given?

Only use qualifiers when necessary. Words are weapons, so choose your weapons wisely. The following table is a collection of qualifiers to watch for and eliminate when communicating a recommendation to a client.

Instead of	Say
I suggest	I recommend
This product can	This product will
If we sign an agreement	When we sign an agreement
I think I can help you.	I know/I'm confident I can help you.
You should try this.	You need to try this.
I'd like to/I want to show you.	I'm going to show you.
You could/should	You need/must
I feel	I know
I hope	I will
I might	I will/can/absolutely
Perhaps/maybe/sorta	Will/is

7. *Client questions are not discovered and resolved.*

Clients usually listen to presentations thoughtfully. When they have a question, it is essential for the salesperson to intercept that question and deftly resolve it in order to illustrate her empathy and professionalism. When a salesperson hears a question and doesn't resolve it, she's ignoring the client. Think about it, folks: What are you doing there if you're going to ignore the client?

When questions are asked, take a mental step back. Why has the client asked the question? Do you need to narrow the question down? (This point is discussed more in Chapter 9.) Whatever you need to do, you must resolve the question. It's essential to maintaining your empathy. When you are asked a question, deal with it with as much concern and focus as your own presentation, because to the prospect it truly is more important than your presentation.

The best way, however, to resolve your client's questions is to ask the client confirming questions. Throughout my years of selling I have found that asking confirming questions really helps me determine the level of the client's grasp of my message.

My presentation's primary goal is to fulfill the need articulated by my client during my probing. After the client articulates a need, I ask a question to confirm that I understand that need. After a client describes the challenges she faces, I state them again to confirm that, indeed, these challenges are hampering her. Only now am I ready to deliver my recommendations.

The psychology behind this tact is to illustrate to clients that their primary goal is of paramount importance to me.

Articulating their challenges is essential because it sets up the urgency of my recommendation. It also communicates that I have discovered a solution to what has been challenging them. Asking them to confirm that the goals and challenges I've reiterated are accurate shows that my presentation is 100 percent about them. (I originally learned this methodology from The Executive Technique Company.)

Don't sound arrogant and self absorbed. Plan to bring up specific confirming questions throughout your presentation.

Here are examples of confirming questions that you can use throughout your presentation to illustrate empathy and smoke out a prospect's question that otherwise might hurt you later on if not resolved.

General Confirming Questions

- How does that look?

- Is that clear?

- Does that look good?

- If you had one question about what I've said so far, what would it be?

- Does that make sense?

- Can you see it fitting in with your company?

- Are we ready to proceed?

- How do you feel about that?

- Any question here?

- Do you understand the logic of that idea?

- How does that sound?

- Is that helpful to you?

- How can this work for you?

More Specific Confirming Questions

- Can you see my (company, product, service) fitting into your strategy?

- What questions do you have regarding my last point?

- How do you see this piece of our recommendation helping?

- Which way are you leaning at this point?

- If you were deciding today, which way would you go? Why?

8. *It wasn't rehearsed.*

There is a great German adage: *Übung. Übung macht den Meister*—Practice. Practice makes the master.

Practice your presentations. You don't have to rehearse out loud each time, but what you must do is be crystal clear about your content and what transitions you will make throughout your presentation to connect that content to your prospect's needs. You also must prepare for where your prospect will have a question or concern during your presentation and craft appropriate responses. Forecasting where a prospect's questions may arise is essential to being perceived as thorough and confident.

Remember the following:

- Before a meeting, anticipate tough questions and write the answers down.

- Trust yourself with the answer you deliver. If you don't know the answer, say so and then arrange a specific time to get back to them.

- Rephrase each question before you answer.

- Be ready to drill down on a client's question or objection to fully understand their concerns, and then respond accordingly.

- Trial close throughout your presentation. At the conclusion of your response, always follow up with a trial close such as, "Do you understand my rationale here?" or "Does this work for you?"

- Remain positive and full of alacrity—cheerful readiness. Never get defensive. Stay personable and tactful.

- Envision yourself as a teacher. You are teaching people what they need to know.

- Monitor your body language. Look right and act right. It's a big part of how people perceive you.

- Keep your answers brief.

- Engage your client to stay aware of their thinking, know when they get it and when they're confused, and then tailor your presentation accordingly.

And keep the following in mind:

- People buy people first and product second.
- Understand that your first role is as a problem solver genuinely committed to earning the client's respect.
- Prove you can add value.
- Never sell what you can't deliver.
- Never be argumentative.
- Know when to back off.
- Always solve the client's primary objective before moving to your own personal recommendations.
- Never patronize.
- Find ways to make the client look good to the boss.

STEVE BUSTS MURPHY

Handing out your presentation in text form detracts from what you are saying. If the text is so important, you could have just e-mailed it to the client. Don't give out your presentation ahead of time. There should be only one presentation paper, the one in your hands. If you feel compelled to keep everyone up to speed using printed handouts, give them your presentation one page at a time so that they stay on track with you. If they ask for the whole copy at once, request at the start of your meeting that everyone moves at your pace for best understanding.

BOTTOM LINE

Rehearse first, present second.

THE COACH WAS WRONG; THERE IS AN "I" IN "TEAM"

MURPHY STRIKES

My colleagues and I were doing swimmingly during a group presentation, handing off gracefully, and not stepping on each other's toes. Then one of my team volunteers that we'd be able to guarantee that no one else in the region would be selling the same product we were offering this client. It was totally off base. How could I have corrected the information without leaving egg on my colleague's face?

When making a presentation as part of a group, each individual has to assume responsibility not just for what they do, but for what everyone else on the team does too. Before the meeting, determine who will lead the meeting. Arrange to rehearse the meeting ahead of time. Decide who on the team presents what, who will field which questions, and establish segues for each presenter for seamless handoffs.

The following is a list of team tips:

- Insist to your colleagues that, together, you rehearse the presentation—and not in the client's parking lot.

- Determine who will deliver each area of the presentation. Assign roles. Know your role and the roles of your colleagues.

- Review possible questions. Decide who in the group will answer specific questions (it's better than letting one person be the know-it-all).

- Before the meeting begins, remind the team that you all look bad if any one of you cannibalizes the other's thoughts. Commit to making each other look good.

- Establish an agenda for the group.

- Avoid too many participants.

- Pick who the quarterback will be and let that person lead.

- Don't add color to what a colleague has just said if it doesn't add to the information. This isn't *Monday Night Football* and you're not Dennis Miller.

- Arrange a postmortem after the meeting and decide on the next steps needed.

STEVE BUSTS MURPHY

Correcting a colleague in front of a client breaks the momentum of a presentation and makes both client and colleague uncomfortable. First off, be sure that you are right and your colleague is wrong. Then determine the gravity of the error. Can it be overlooked for now? (The product comes in 21 colors, not 22.) Or is it something so severe that it needs to be corrected now? (There is no guarantee of exclusivity.)

Before the meeting, agree on a code phrase that will be used if someone on the team makes a mistake that needs correcting at the moment. After your colleague's error, your next statement could begin with the code phrase "it's also important for us to notice" and then add some clarifying information. The code words would be your teammate's cue to acknowledge and correct the error himself. "Say, I may have misspoken when I mentioned exclusivity. Let me make sure of that and get back to you."

BOTTOM LINE

Never correct a colleague during a team presentation. Let small errors slide. Use a code phrase to notify your teammate of an error, and let that colleague correct the mistake.

9

DEFENDING YOUR TURF AGAINST MURPHY

HANDLING CLIENT QUESTIONS

A large, international corporation familiar with my work had just completed an in-house, yearlong sales training program for 150 employees. The corporation determined it needed help with quality control, so a representative of the corporation called me and said the corporation was looking for someone to serve as a consultant for the program as it entered its next stage. It sounded like an ideal client, one perfect for my expertise.

But, between me and the job stood five executives—seated, actually, around a boardroom table that was about to become a dinner table, and I was the main course.

It wasn't that I expected my pitch to be a walk in the park, but I wasn't prepared for the bombardment they had in store. The five executives not only had questions about what I might bring to the job, they were openly skeptical, each voicing serious concerns about my ability to handle the task at hand. With each objection, I probed to pinpoint the concern, and then set about to enthusiastically answer it. But, they were relentless and, I repeat, there were five of them.

Each executive considered his concerns to be of utmost significance and felt no shyness in expressing his concerns. I'm used to toughing out the toughest situations, but these five had me on the run until finally it hit me: "Whoa! I'm close to blowing this!" Suddenly I realized it wasn't just me and five intense businessmen at the table. Now, Murphy was sitting in too.

Then, I got a grip. I told myself, "Wait a minute! I've spent 20 hours studying this client's situation. I have trained over 30,000 executives in sales. I have interviewed everyone at this table at length. No one can coach these 150 salespeople better than me!"

Sometimes there comes a point where you must summon the presence of your professionalism, your courage, and your abilities and quietly resolve to yourself that you were meant to sell. People ask questions for many reasons: ego, fear, completing their due diligence, testing you, and more. Whatever the reason, you still have to answer—with confidence. It's confidence based on the fact that you're there because you have something important to offer.

Clients aren't asking questions to amuse themselves; they honestly want to know the answer. It's not about your ego. It's about your knowledge. Face the music, and answer the questions. You'll eventually win your clients' respect and business.

For these five executives, I turned the situation around by reminding myself of my own abilities. I decided to answer the questions as if I already had been hired. It allowed me to gain control and focus on the answers. I earned these executives' respect and the position.

THEY'RE NOT PICKING ON YOU; THEY'RE ASKING QUESTIONS

MURPHY STRIKES

Most of my clients act professionally, but I had one recently who was a real nasty, negative piece of work. I have a good product and gave an intelligent presentation, but he looked right past that and, instead, seemed to enjoy trying to make me squirm with sarcastic and snide questions like "This is supposed to solve all my problems." "So, your plan is a magic bullet?" "You're going to tell me this is the best thing since sliced bread?" (That's right, sarcastic and unimaginative.) He was working my last nerve, and I delivered every answer while biting my tongue. How could I have gotten him off his high horse short of a well-deserved right hook?

As salespeople and communicators we must first understand the essence and meaning of questions in business. At its core, this is what makes or breaks our success—a most important point in controlling Murphy.

Questions from customers, prospects, and clients are requests for more information, *not an attack on your ability or the ability of your product*. Questions asked by clients are not meant to debunk your idea, they are asked to better understand your message. Your understanding of your product far out-reaches your client's.

It's easy to think in the heat of a sales presentation that we are speaking to people who see our product with our eyes. *They don't.* Clients cannot possibly understand your product as well as you do. They do not deal with it daily. They haven't spent months or years with it. For most, this is their very first brush with it.

Your actions during the questioning phase of a presentation are as essential as what you say. Think of questions as the client's way of saying, "I'm ready to buy your product; just resolve this issue and we're ready to go!" When you train yourself to think this way, your tone and manner of resolving questions becomes more of a collaboration versus a defensive maneuver.

Clients know when you are defensive, and they know when you are supportive. They can feel it, and they can hear it. One wrongly toned word or phrase can bring Murphy front and center into your conversation.

Try this simple experiment: Accompany a colleague on a sales presentation and observe the client asking questions. Watch as your colleague answers. Is it relaxed or anxious, defensive and curt, or excited and thorough?

Turnabout is fair play, so then have your colleague accompany you. Share the information and what you've observed.

What happens during a question-and-answer session indicates the entire sales process in a nutshell.

STEVE BUSTS MURPHY

When it comes to an irritable, angry, or snide client, let me say it again, rule number one in sales is *never take it personally.*

First off, be thankful that you're not married to this guy, and then realize that you are dealing with a very jaded, negative fellow. When someone comes at you with attitude, you need to address it. A grounded salesperson, one who is mature and confident, acknowledges this type of behavior by sincerely asking, "Jim, are you okay today?" Wait for a response. If he says, "Sure, why?" then dig further. "It feels as though the issues we're discussing are somewhat hopeless or unrealistic to you. Is that so?" Ask, "Have there been previous situations similar to these that have backfired?" Wait for his responses.

Then say: "It's important for you to know that my belief is that we can solve the issues you've brought up quite successfully, but I'm feeling as though I might be guilty by association from past backfires. Am I right?" Wait for his response.

Get the strategy here? When your intuition says that a client's comments are unfounded, smoke them out. Ask a series of open-ended questions, delivered with empathy, to pinpoint the anxiety. Give a grouch plenty of room to vent and then get it all out. *Then* you have an open space to reestablish your meeting agenda and get his agreement to proceed. By doing this you also regain control of the meeting—and his behavior—and move forward.

BOTTOM LINE

Don't take clients' negative personality quirks personally. Avoid playing into the negativity by pinpointing real reasons for the bad attitude—the facts of the matter. You may not be able to resolve a bad attitude, but you can resolve those issues.

THE ANSWER TO UNDERSTANDING QUESTIONS

MURPHY STRIKES

After my presentation, the client asked me a number of questions about one of her competitors, knowing that this competitor is also my client. I attempted to skirt the questions with remarks such as "I'm sure you understand that I can't divulge proprietary information." After saying she entirely understood, she came back with remarks such as "Hey, you say you're here to help me out, so give me some information that will really help me out." I said what I could, but my discomfort level was so high after the meeting I felt like I needed to rinse. What should I do when the questions wander into the inappropriate?

No guidelines can prepare you for every possibility when it comes to client questions. There are as many ways for a question to come your way as there are clients. Still, by understanding these 10 basics, you'll be ready to face the vast majority of questions you'll be asked. These are not rules, only guidelines for how to approach whatever may be asked.

THE TEN FUNDAMENTALS OF QUESTIONS

Understanding the nature of questions can be boiled down to:

1. Clients want information. Don't take their questions personally.

2. When asked a question, increase your empathy.

3. Anticipate client questions before the meeting and resolve them ahead of time.

4. Answer all questions, but only when appropriate.

5. When you resolve questions, you are a teacher.

6. Clarify general questions to pinpoint your response.

7. Use confirming questions to verify that clients understand and accept your answers.

8. Make your answers concise.

9. Make eye contact and other physical movements that convey confidence and empathy.

10. Be in charge of yourself; be in charge of your answers.

Clients want information. Don't take their questions personally.

Often, clients must sell your recommendation to someone else. And they often need additional information to defend your idea to their superiors, when you won't be there. They ask questions to resolve in their own minds the benefits of your product to help them gain confidence in accepting it themselves. Sometimes it's just plain due diligence on their part, because suddenly they realize that they're ready to make a decision to go with your product or service right now, something they originally had no intention of doing.

Client questions are a particularly delicate stage of the presentation because so much can go wrong. It's a time when Murphy is never too far away. He's waiting for you to become defensive, to cave in, to misunderstand the question and deliver the wrong answer. He's dying for you to gloss over a question so he can whisper into your client's ear that you really don't care about the client's issues, you just want the sale.

Consider the analogy of the concerned, calm doctor answering questions from his patient versus the distracted doctor who briefly answers his patient's questions because, after all, he's got other patients and a one o'clock tee-off. When I made rounds with my father as a boy, I was always impressed with his bedside manner. When he visited a patient, he concentrated only on that patient's well being, such as understanding post-surgery progress. His demeanor was calm as he offered empathy and encouragement. Sometimes he would pull a pen and paper from his pocket and quietly draw the actual operation on a piece of paper for the patient, outlining the exact veins, arteries, ligaments, and organs that were to be part of the operation. He would ask questions to ensure that the patient understood what he was drawing and what he was saying. He'd carefully watch for facial movements or other indications to pick up worries or fears and address them so that the patient could have positive thinking going into surgery.

You are that doctor. You have to be concerned. You have to detail your intentions and have the client agree that your plans will be beneficial. You seek much more than a sale. You want a partnership that's based on respect for the client.

How will you know that clients accept your collaborative effort? When they accept your product.

When asked a question, increase your empathy.

When clients ask a question, whether it's during your presentation or at the end, this is the time to engage them. Get excited about the opportunity to clear something up. Illustrate your knowledge and your understanding of the client's situation. Reinforce the link between your product and the problem you unearthed during your probing and resolve the challenge that your clients themselves have already acknowledged.

Reinforcement is necessary because usually your client has forgotten what that gap really was. Calmly remind the client that the reason that you're here is because, according to the client, a problem needs fixing.

But, at the same time you have to empathize with the client. Maybe she has sticker-shock. Maybe he's worried about the ease of implementing your solution. Maybe it boils down to worries about selling it to the boss. You must clearly and thoroughly resolve each question that the client asks and link it back to the gap that the two of you mutually agreed upon. Your empathy is vital.

Anticipate client questions before the meeting and resolve them ahead of time.

One reason practice is so important is because you never know exactly what a client will ask. (And, by the way, it's really better that way. The mystery and unknown add the spice. If it were all predictable, you'd be bored out of your brain.) No, you're not sure what's going to happen. So what? This is the real world. Get with it. So, anticipate likely questions as you design your presentation and then prepare responses.

List potential questions your client might have as you design your presentation. Then, prioritize them from the client's perspective. Start with the one most likely to be paramount to them, the second, third, and so on. Then, *resolve these questions during the presentation*. If you're sensitive to the client, you should know whether or not the questions needed answering. "Just so you know, our return policy is no questions asked for returns within 60 days." Resolving potential questions during your presentation avoids allowing the client to sense any ill-preparedness on your part or insensitivity to her needs. Kick Murphy out the door before he sets one foot in!

Write out all your questions, including the inane. I once listed out as many questions as I could possibly conceive of before a meeting with a financial services company, including this one from as far afield as I could think of: "Would you be available to do some of the selling for us and maybe entertain becoming head of sales for us in time?"

It was the wildest, most unlikely question I could think of. They asked it.

Planning for this question was critical because I wanted to answer professionally and with empathy, completely free of aloofness (you can imagine how a surprise question like this might bring on a case of sudden modesty or stammering or any number of clumsy responses). But, I was ready. I knew I needed to bring the client back to the original value I was providing for the company and have the client realize that hiring me would, in time, work against the company's original goal of hiring an outside consultant.

The title of Art Linkletter's TV show, *Kids Say the Darnedest Things*, can be easily reworked into, "Clients ask the darnedest things." When you believe that nothing can come up that you haven't anticipated, realize that Murphy is halfway in the door. Creating and answering client questions before your presentation lets you think about your best responses and make them client focused and relaxed when you provide an answer. When the client asks, even if it's at the very start of your presentation, there's no whammy involved. You actually enjoy it: You expected the question and know the answer. My, you're looking good!

Answer all questions, but only when appropriate.

You're reading right. The time to answer questions isn't always at the moment they're asked. This is a decision you need to make based on what's best for the edification of your client.

If your client asks a question at the start of your presentation that you know should not be answered until you have covered two other points ("So, how is this going to translate to improved sales?"), and covering of these two points will significantly help resolve that question, then your job is to state that there are two other issues that are important to cover before this question is answered. Emphasize that covering them will help with the answer. Confirm that that's okay.

Asking for an okay retains your consultative, empathetic relationship. They need to agree with you before you continue. It evidences that you've prepared data in a correct sequence, one that will help them make an informed decision. It also keeps you in control of the meeting.

When you answer questions, you are a teacher.

Think of your favorite teacher—whether the teacher was from grade school, middle school, high school, college, postgraduate work, or a family member. Describe this teacher in three words. What comes to mind: clear, thoughtful, enthusiastic, patient, fair? Think of yourself as that teacher when you resolve clients' questions. Embody those qualities.

A while back I was in the middle of closing a client on a training series for the client's salespeople. Throughout our meetings, I noticed what I took to be a bit of skepticism as to the final outcome and benefit of the seminars I was proposing. After a while of listening to my sales intuition, I chose to confront my client and ask about the vibe I was getting.

But, first I had to remind myself, "Okay, Stevo, make this question sound 100 percent genuine and, at the same time, enthusiastic to really get at the issue of the skepticism." It was an important state of mind to reach, and I did it by recalling

Nick, my first sales manager in the life insurance industry back in 1977.

Nick was one of the finest teachers I ever had in business. He was clear, concise, compelling, and enthusiastic. As I prepared to confront my client's perceived reluctance, I pictured him in my mind and asked the client, "Deborah, can you see the benefit of what I'm offering, the opportunity to demonstrably professionalize your salespeople?" She responded, "My real concern is the training of their sales manager in order to perpetuate the systems you'll be creating."

That was exactly what I needed to hear in order to address her remaining skepticism. After asking my client several questions about the proficiency of her sales manager, I realized that I needed to provide a training program specifically for the manager, in addition to the manager's staff. As I reflected on this situation, I realized that what moved my client forward was my ability to create a comfortable enough setting for her to volunteer her concern for the training of her sales manager. That would not have happened if I ignored that skepticism. Nor would it have happened had I not reached into my own personal, positive experiences with a "teacher" I trusted to serve as a guide on approaching this challenge.

Clarify general questions to pinpoint your response.
Most client questions in business require distillation down to specifics. You must qualify generalized questions before any realistic resolution is possible.

During a stay at Long Island's magnificent Eastern End, I visited an upscale gourmet grocery. At the checkout I handed the owner my American Express card. The cashier, by chance the owner, promptly said, "Oh, we don't accept Amex, only MasterCard and Visa." My first thought (after my years of experience with American Express sales executives) was that the owner didn't understand the value of accepting this card. I asked the owner why, and he said because the rate was way too high.

But, this response was much too general. I asked what he thought the rate was. He guessed 8 or 9 percent, much higher than the actual discount rate. I explained the benefits of reevaluating his acceptance, given his upscale clientele and the fact that those card users charge significantly more on Amex cards per purchase. He agreed to see an Amex representative and now accepts the card quite happily.

Clients often operate out of a different understanding of your product or service. So you must resolve that misunderstanding by pinpointing the lack of understanding. But, before you can get to that point, you have to accept the possibility (and make no mistake, this requires *humility*) that, despite your estimation that you have covered a certain point in question at least three times, your client still doesn't get it.

Pause. Look in the mirror. Acknowledge which aspect of this issue you haven't been clear about. Forget your frustration. Move forward by resolving the issue to your client's satisfaction.

Use confirming questions to verify that clients understand and accept your answers.

How do you know that the issue in question has been resolved? It will make the difference in whether or not Murphy shows up again later on in the discussion. In most cases you can resolve the issue by asking clients, plainly, if they understand the answer you've just put forth.

Dig a little. Find out if your client understands the answer, but also examine how he answers. Is his response credible? Did you get a lukewarm "okay"? If so, respectfully challenge it by asking another confirming question, and then another if necessary, until you're confident your client understands and accepts your answer.

You build your presentation point upon point. Any misunderstood point is a chink in your armor, a weak spot in your foundation.

A few months ago I was meeting with the president of a magazine group. I told her I needed her agreement that her sales team could only be made strong and effective through a systematized selling process. But, she was worried. "My account managers won't be on automatic from this process, will they?" she asked.

"No not at all," I replied, "In fact, being versed in this selling system will have them be more client tailored than their current method allows." I then proceeded to answer her question by illustrating my recommended selling system and how the training would be tailored to the value proposition of their specific client groups. Once I finished with this explanation, I asked, "Are you beginning to see the importance of systematizing your selling process for your account managers?" She nodded yes, but my intuition told me this response was not sufficient for me to continue with my presentation. I needed assurance that she accepted my methodology.

I then asked, "Can you see that through this system your account managers will be more sophisticated in their selling efforts? By using this method they will be able to put much more of their time into client preparation and probing. Do you see how this will make their presentations 100 percent tailored for each individual client?"

She replied, "Yes, now I see that the system that you will be building will be ours and ours alone and how it will benefit our client."

Now I was ready to move on. I needed to hear her say the actual words that she understood my point and I had. I was ready to build from this point forward the balance of my recommendation knowing that she understood the outcome of our meeting.

See the list of confirming questions from Chapter 8 to further understand the benefit of using them to underscore your sincerity in resolving questions and also to be sure your clients have understood and accepted your answer.

Make your answers concise.

More is not better. Naturally concise answers come when you are prepared for them. No hemming, hawing, or superfluous yammer. Concise responses make you sound knowledgeable, but only if you're prepared for the question. You can't predict every question, but you can get a good idea from your probing meetings which issues you'll have to respond to.

Conciseness also gives your client the opportunity to ask you another question that needs to be resolved versus getting off track by a verbose answer. When you go off on a tangent, you create more work for yourself by adding data that doesn't need to be there. Excess data turns clients off and creates doubt, which you will then have to overcome. In other words, unnecessary information only increases your workload.

Still, remain flexible when responding to a client. You may give a perfectly adequate concise response to your client, yet he may feel you did not resolve his question. Be ready at all times to read your clients as you respond to them. If a client looks confused or uncertain from your response, ask if your response resolved the question.

Don't assume everything's all right and don't paper over your own sales intuition if you get the feeling the answer didn't connect. Often a client won't ask you to further resolve that issue. She will probably let it go, but she'll make a mental note that the issue is still unresolved until it's time to close the sale and then she'll bring it up again.

Hi, Murphy! What kept you?

Make eye contact and other physical movements that convey confidence and empathy.

The bulk of most communication is weighed in the context of its physical delivery. Maintain eye contact with clients when they ask questions and when you respond. I often observe that salespeople look away the moment they are asked a question. This automatically puts Murphy center stage telling your client that you are not sure of yourself or the answer you're about to give. You may not notice, but the client will.

Solid eye contact is essential for communicating confidence and empathy in your answer. Be aware of your body language when you are resolving questions. Are you genuinely engaged in your answer or does your posture or movement signify a defensive position?

Be in charge of yourself; be in charge of your answers.

Clients know when someone is on autopilot and when someone is genuinely engaged. They can't be won over by a smile or a skimpy, short response when a thorough answer delivered with empathy is what's required. Clients base an enormous amount of their decision on how they are treated. They may be high maintenance, needing you to play the role of patient consultant who soothes them before they agree to a purchase. Don't let Murphy muck up an otherwise great presentation by short-changing your client with a lack of honest, self-confident enthusiasm and dedication.

Years ago a dear friend told me that in dealing with people one must give, love, and always serve. When selling, always give people your knowledge and understanding. Show love by being patient and humble. Serve clients as if you were the client.

What goes on inside you and how you manage those feelings are as important as what you manifest on the outside. You will keep Murphy away by controlling both.

STEVE BUSTS MURPHY

You're ready for the client's questions, but she asks something entirely inappropriate, in this case proprietary information about a direct competitor. You want to score points, but you have to maintain your ethics. It's a challenge, but it can be done.

First question to ask yourself, "When I mention that this type of disclosure is unprofessional, does she agree?" My guess is that you never sought this type of agreement. When something is clearly a breach of professionalism, it's a fact that both of you can acknowledge, so make sure she acknowledges it.

Second, discern a client's patterns. When a client goes on and on about the competition to the point of seeking proprietary information, you need to control the situation before it controls you. Set the ground rules very matter-of-factly.

Joan, your desire for information about Acme, Inc., is understandable, but I'm sure you know it's confidential. Can you appreciate that if I were meeting with my client at Acme, I would not reveal our conversations either?

Wait for a response. Do not continue until you've gotten her agreement on this point. Too often we move forward and we don't close the issue.

Finally, begin to assess whether you want to continue a relationship with a client that refuses to let the issue go. Someone who openly displays a lack of ethics could well turn the tables on you.

BOTTOM LINE

Stand up to inappropriate questions by stating, calmly and clearly, how and why the query is inappropriate. Confirm that the client understands. A pattern of unethical behavior on the part of the client, even if directed at others, may portend trouble ahead for you.

SPLIT-SECOND THINKING

MURPHY STRIKES

My client has plenty of money, but when I opened it up for questions she surprised me by asking, "What can I get for free?" I went in to make a sale, and I was suddenly put in a position of dealing with a charity case. The fact was I had nothing for free, yet felt like I should toss a bone. Was it possible to reply in the positive and still be truthful?

How do you deal with whammy questions out of nowhere? It requires split-second thinking, responses that are honest, assured, and betray no lack of confidence.

The questions and objections range from "That's impossible!" to "That's not the way we do things around here!" to "Aren't you guys all the same?" Whatever it is, you need to be ready.

Split-second thinking doesn't mean spitting out the first thing that comes to mind. It's far from it. First, you need to collect your thoughts and begin to formulate your response. To gain that extra time either repeat or rephrase your client's question. Repeating or rephrasing a question also puts you back in control by accepting the question as your own through your reiteration.

This, importantly, is not simply repeating a question back to someone like a child at a spelling bee restating every word that's asked. Nobody wants to listen to a parrot. But, it does mean repeating the essence of the question to be sure you're on the right track.

For example, when the client offers a pop surprise question on scheduling by asking:

How long will the whole process take if we train all our managers in every branch?

you should respond with:

The length of the process depends on a number of factors, but in your case I'm expecting a total of 3 months for each branch. The entire schedule, of course, depends on how many branches we train simultaneously.

It's deceptively simple. By asking the question aloud in your own words, you give yourself a moment to collect your thoughts, honestly consider your reply, and stay in control.

If the question is more complex, a slightly different tact comes into play. A client once said to me:

The last time we did training, my salespeople used what they learned but then forgot it. It was like the flavor of the month. How will my salespeople keep the technology that you teach them throughout their selling efforts, given the uncertainty of our times and the significant pressure they're under this year to produce their numbers?

I responded:

What are the fundamental differences between your past training efforts and this selling system? The difference is that this system will be perpetuated by your managers and the sales management systems they will use throughout this year to quantify your results from the system.

In this case, I rephrased the question in a way that narrowed the objection not to simply the world of selling systems, but to a comparison between my system and the one before. In the original questions, I was being asked to defend an entire system that was not my responsibility and one I was not prepared to defend. My rephrasing left me with only having to defend my own system, which I was fully prepared to do.

We've discussed the importance of knowing the types of questions that you'll be asked during a presentation. This shows a depth of knowledge about your client and how much you care about helping the client. It's now important to monitor the length of your responses. There are certain questions that can be resolved with one or two words. There are other questions that involve a more thorough response. Have your responses timed when you rehearse your answers.

If you need to, use a Dictaphone to record your responses and play them back. The value of this is that you hear your response as your client would hear it. Is it too short or is it too long? Is it too simple or is it too complex? Did you truly answer the question?

Remember, you are expecting someone to listen to your answers. How easy is it for you to listen to your answers?

STEVE BUSTS MURPHY

You go into a sales meeting to make a sale, but your client turns into a charity case, expecting freebies as a normal part of doing business even though you're not prepared to give out anything for free. Is it possible to reply in the positive and still be truthful?

Absolutely not. Gain the client's understanding and agreement on what you can and cannot offer. You must be ethical as a professional and responsible to your company. It's tough to not give in ("I suppose I could cut my commission . . ."), but the moment you do Murphy comes with you. You are not the attorney for the client, you are the advocate of your company and the products it markets. The benefits of your product or services are reward enough for your client.

BOTTOM LINE

Honestly tell your client what you can and can't do. You cannot be asked to do anything more than be fair. Never shortchange yourself or your company.

COUNTERPUNCHING

MURPHY STRIKES

As a salesperson, I want to sell value, but throughout my presentation, my client kept bugging me about "How much is this going to cost?" and "Just give me the bottom line." I wanted to get through my presentation before discussing prices, but he was so adamant I felt evasive. What could I have done?

Most objections can be summed up in two phrases: "I don't have the time" or "I don't have the money." The moment your client voices objections, it's one of the most volatile times of the meeting.

You can't just roll your eyes and give the client a good shake on the shoulders (however much you may want to). You must meet the objections as they arise. One easy way to do this is to be ready for the most commonly raised issues with quick, but meaningful responses that clear the objection and keep you in control.

Here's a list of objections—including time and money—I've heard raised countless times, as well as recommendations for handling each.

It's just too much money. You should have gotten sufficient knowledge of money issues during your probing to not be thrown here, but if this one comes early, ask, "Compared to what? What was the amount budgeted for this? What had you planned to invest?"

We don't have the time. Handle this by asking, "Which aspect of the recommendation seems too time-consuming for you? Let's review your objectives and quantify the time required to discover if the time investment is greater than or less than the benefit of the solution."

It doesn't look right for us. If you were asking confirming questions throughout your meetings, this should not come up; still this doubt can be pinpointed and resolved by first asking, "Which part of the recommendation doesn't fit?"

This looks way too complicated. Respond by asking, "Let's review the critical path that needs to be followed and resolve which parts need to be simplified."

This will never fly with the boss. Respond by asking, "Which parts would your boss reject? Let's list them and pinpoint the issues with each; that way we can see how to present this to your boss in the best light."

We've been burned before. Respond by asking, "Which part of the recommendation are you leery about? This is essential for me to know before we move forward, because if you get burned, I get fried."

My current supplier is good enough. It is rare that this would come up after a probing meeting, because by now you should have determined that the status quo is anything but good enough. Say, "Let's review how the recommendation here compares to your current supplier's role. I believe that this recommendation strengthens your position, particularly from what we discovered earlier."

We do just fine right now. Respond by asking, "We agreed earlier that you wanted to improve your current situation. Has that changed since our last meeting?"

It's too risky. Respond by asking, "Which part appears too risky? Let's examine it to establish a fail-safe mechanism for this program so we eliminate that risk."

STEVE BUSTS MURPHY

Even when all a client talks about is cost, the real concern is usually not cost, but profit. Your clients want to make money. And what you're selling has value because it will make money for them—not because it's necessarily the cheapest, but because it brings the best return. Keep them focused on how your product or idea will bring them that profit.

When a client goes to price, *they see no value!* (Give a tip of the hat to *Getting to Yes* by Roger Fisher and William Ury on this one.) When clients see no value, what you have to offer gets homogenized with every one of your competitors. The key to avoiding the trap of discussing price too soon is to thoroughly understand the needs and interests of your clients (quality, value, profits) and show that throughout your presentation.

Specifically, when your client insisted on prices, you could have responded, "It's obvious you're concerned about your budget. I believe what I have will benefit your bottom line nicely, but I feel I need to lay out my proposal so that you can see clearly how that will work. By the time I complete the presentation, I'm sure you'll be very pleased with how it all adds up for your bottom line."

BOTTOM LINE

Concerns about money and costs usually mean concerns about profits. Concentrate on the value of what you offer, not its cost. Emphasize how its value will bring more profitability to the client.

10

CLOSES THAT
CLOSE OUT MURPHY

---

*It had been a painstaking 2 days. One of the world's largest
banks had called me in to train 10 executives from the corporate finance department. In back-to-back sessions from
nine in the morning until the end of the afternoon on both
days, we practiced many of the techniques detailed in
this book. My clients took turns acting in the roles of salesperson and client, testing their colleagues. We analyzed
individual approaches, videotaped mock sales calls, and
critiqued them.*

*After nearly 20 years of these sorts of seminars, I'm able to
give myself an honest assessment of the success of my program and, I'm happy to say, I was feeling good about our
progress. As I do at the conclusion of many of my seminars,
I asked each participant to give me a summary of how he or*

she felt we had done. I was pleased to find positive reports from all 10 executives.

At the end of the 2 days, it was time for me to meet with their boss, a high-level player in the company whose attitude wasn't exactly congenial. Just as I began to debrief him on our sessions, ranging from our overall results to the progress of each executive, I noticed him giving me a withering look. Well, maybe "glaring" is a more accurate way to describe it.

"I suppose you're going to tell me how great you are?" he challenged. It was a Murphy moment, a moment when you want to say, "As a matter of fact, pal, I am great!" But, that would have brought me down to his level of communication—challenge and counterchallenge—with no chance for me to come out on top.

Instead, I let the facts speak for themselves.

"Actually, what I'd like to do is take you through the comments that the 10 people I trained gave about the program," I said calmly, without a trace of being rattled. "After we've looked at that, you can decide for yourself whether or not the training was a success." I let the glowing reports do the talking.

This wasn't a sales close in the traditional sense, but it served the same purpose. It was the time when we reviewed what had gone before and I prepared to naturally move to a close that let the client self-realize the benefit of what I had to offer.

The client became convinced, but I did not convince him. I showed him facts and let him convince himself.

"**G**reat is the art of beginning," a philosopher once said, but added, "greater still is the art of ending." Your opening remarks and agenda prepare the way, your probing determines your link to the client, your presentation explains why you are there, and your question-and-answer period clears up doubts. Your close ties it all together and, literally, seals the deal (although it may take several meetings before a contract is signed).

Closing a sales presentation is an art form. It requires humanity and listening. Closings fail because a salesperson assumed something that wasn't there. Closings begin with your opening comments and shadow the presentation through all of its parts until it's time to determine the next step that two people should naturally agree upon together.

As we move into our discussion on techniques for successful closing it's important to understand fundamentally that closing is nothing more than the next appropriate step on the road to gaining acceptance for the recommendation you have engineered for your client.

A good formula for closing is:

1. Acknowledge your client's issues from your probing meeting.

2. Gain the client's agreement on those issues.

3. Present your recommendation as a direct result of those agreed-upon issues.

4. Recommend that the client accept your recommendation to resolve those issues.

BE FLEXIBLE. LOOK AHEAD. STAY ALIVE.

MURPHY STRIKES

The sales call was going great. I felt confident enough to think forward to signing a deal. That's when I said something along the lines of "If this works out, I'll treat you to the best bottle of champagne money can buy." The client replied, almost sheepishly, "Probably better not, I'm a recovering alcoholic." I felt like a total ass. Besides not having made the remark in the first place, what could I have done?

Like so many parts of the sales call, flexibility is crucial to a successful close. It's possible that something has occurred in the eleventh hour to deep-six your close. Relax. Figure out what it is and move on!

Always remember to verify what's dear to your clients. The more you do this the more they understand your empathy and intelligence. Think of it as a proposal for marriage. Would you ask someone to marry you with no understanding of the other person's likes and dislikes, lifestyle, etc.? Know your client and you'll know what steps you will take together.

You cannot be tentative with a close. Mel Brooks, the great comedian, writer, and producer said, "Don't tap the bell; ring the bell; we're not going for balance, we're going for thrills!" This has so much meaning to a salesperson. A salesperson is a performer who must ring the bell, not just tap it, to convince the audience—the client. When we sell, and in this case close, we better mean it, we better believe it, and we better show it. Don't expect applause, of course; expect the sale.

Performers understand that they must deliver a great performance each time in order to perform again. Do you? Imagine an actor doing great throughout a play and then letting his performance flag in the closing scene. Closing is the emotional payoff to a great presentation. Why be in sales without it? Where's the fun or self-actualization without this? It takes a cast-iron stomach to sell. It takes a rock-solid constitution to face life every day knowing that with each presentation and close you are putting your own reputation and the reputation of your company on the line. But as long as you're in this line of work, accept it and embrace it.

Nothing can take the place of genuine enthusiasm. For your enthusiasm to score, to be felt by people and move them, it has to have been brewing inside you for days until you see your client. From your opening handshake to your closing statement you must embody someone who is genuinely excited to deliver this great news!

Source your enthusiasm the night before your meeting. You envision the fun—yes, the fun—of presenting your recommendation. Envision your client smiling and breathing a sigh of relief that someone has created an ideal solution for her problem. Move into your close by physically getting exhilarated.

People know when you're jazzed and when you're not. Your presentation begins with that jazzed feeling at your greeting and then fully manifests at your close. I actually can't think of a close with a client in the last 10 years when I haven't genuinely said at the end of my close, "This would really be a lot of fun to do."

Wrap up with a sense of elation. What you've done in your sales meeting was a good thing, even a great thing—and now that confidence will translate to your closing. It's not just another notch in their rifle ("Got that out of the way!"). It also makes it a lot easier to get out of bed the next morning and look at yourself in the mirror.

Leave the meeting positively and with a clear head. This means enthusiastically articulating the next step in the selling process with a plan that proves you are eager and happy to take the next steps.

Paint the horizon for your clients. Closings should center on the opportunity that your recommendation offers about the future. Speak to your clients from the clearest future they can relate to. They in turn will understand the value of your recommendation as you articulate that future, providing they see your recommendation bringing them that future.

During your greeting and tailored small talk you are observing your client and sensing the level of receptivity to you as a person first. Then you observe the reaction to your eventual content. When you present your agenda, you look for the level of understanding and agreement to the agenda. As you deliver your proposal, you observe the level of assimilation of the information you have crafted and simultaneously gauge the level of excitement and desire for your recommendation.

That same search for agreement and understanding from your client is at the heart of the close. Closings fail when you change or lose focus. The moment you forget or move your focus somewhere other than directly on your client, Murphy automatically slips into your place and begins selling for you.

I was once hired to coach a salesperson specifically on his closing abilities. Throughout our day together I noticed that an important reason why it was difficult for him to close his clients was not because he wasn't prepared or articulate, it was because there was no connection of humanity or relationship being forged between him and his clients. At the start of each meeting he would begin by asking his clients how they were, while looking into his briefcase and taking out his sales material. I could see a lack of relationship at the very beginning of each meeting and a lack of connection throughout the meeting.

You must show engagement at the very start of your meeting, in the middle of your meeting, and at the end of your meeting to hope to close successfully. It's what I call your warmth factor. Have you created a climate of easy give-and-take discussion throughout your meeting, or have you focused your attention on just delivering your message regardless of its receptivity?

STEVE BUSTS MURPHY

These days, business is fraught with personal pressures and issues—past and present—for all of us. The heart of your mistake was that you made an assumption, and whether it's about drinking, politics, or anything else, don't make guesses about your client. It would have been much better to begin the offer by asking, "Do you like champagne?" Once the mistake is made, of course, a quick apology and a shift of gears to a luncheon offer should suffice. "Oh, sorry about that. No offense intended. How about lunch at your favorite restaurant instead?"

When you state the future, play it safe and be aspirational. Consider how you might have offered something along the lines of, "As this begins to work out and we deliver on the results we've established together, let's celebrate. How about a great, fun lunch on me? You pick the place!" By the way, besides showing generosity and enthusiasm, offers such as these also test your client. After making the offer, watch to see how the client reacts. If the immediate reaction to your initial offer is favorable, listen to the level of enthusiasm. If you feel genuine excitement, jump on it. Pull your calendar out and plan the lunch right then and there.

Is the response lukewarm? If the client doesn't pick up on it, let it go for now. You can always revisit it later, after the results are in and your job has been completed. "By the way, I'm ready for you to take me up on that lunch offer." Don't push, but restate the offer to indicate your sincerity and openness ("When it's good for you, we'll do it!").

BOTTOM LINE

Don't assume anything about your client. Let offers of generosity be open to acceptance or refusal without any expectations—it is, after all, an offer not a demand. When you offer lunch, game tickets, golf, and the like, however, listen carefully to the response. This can prove an effective gauge of your client's enthusiasm about the sales call.

HAVE FORBEARANCE; IT PAYS

MURPHY STRIKES

My message is substantial and can't be squeezed down to just one meeting, even if I have an hour. Yet, more often than I'd care to mention a client has said, "Look, this is your one shot!" Part of me wants to jump to the challenge, but I also don't feel like being forced into a quick draw. Going one way may get the part and the other may get me booted. Which part of my brain should I follow?

It's now time to close your meeting, but that does not mean it's time to close the client. *Don't sell too soon*. It's easy to begin making recommendations too early with clients. But waiting lets you establish a relationship with the client. *This is where the bonding occurs*.

A common myth of sales meetings—even among salespeople!—is that they follow a trajectory like an arrow that flies in a straight, tidy line from greeting to sale. It can work that way, but not usually. One of the most strategic weapons at your service is patience.

A successful close does not necessarily mean a sale. A successful close could be the uncovering of one key issue, essential to closing, that must be resolved before a client says yes. The uncovering of this issue brings you closer to a correct sale and closer to your client. (Of course, there are certainly times when the first meeting may be your one and only shot at a sale. In some industries, especially for those people who sell ad space for magazines, the meeting is *the* meeting. If you don't make a convincing pitch in that first round, you aren't coming back. In those cases it isn't possible to wait. This is your one opportunity. Take advantage of it.)

If it is at all possible, wait to make the sale until the second, third, or fourth call. Consider this information from the National Research Bureau:

> A recent survey among sales executives revealed that 80 percent of all sales are made after the fifth call, but 48 percent of salespeople call once and give up; 25 percent call twice and quit; 12 percent make three calls and stop; and 5 percent give up after the fourth call. Only 10 percent keep on calling. And, it is this 10 percent—one salesperson in ten—that makes 80 percent of the sales.

The key word here is *forbearance*. If I could copyright that word, I would. It's an essential element of staying in control. Forbearance means to restrain yourself, to abstain, to keep yourself in control. *Webster's New World Dictionary* describes it as "patient restraint." You want to close that sale so bad, but you have to resist. You must patiently restrain yourself. Develop a rapport over several meetings. It is best for everyone involved. The more extensive the relationship that you develop, the more intelligence and humanity you'll be able to reveal (and comprehend).

By waiting, you have the opportunity to truly handle a client's needs. Too many people only uncover some of a client's needs before closing versus uncovering all the needs. By exercising forbearance you illustrate to your client thoughtfulness and patience. You also have the opportunity for more success for yourself because what you sell will more closely match what the client needs. Let the client know that at the beginning of the meeting, when you state your agenda.

When we're through today, we'll take a look at how things stand and decide what our next steps should be.

STEVE BUSTS MURPHY

You're eager to make that sale and can almost taste it, but your better judgment tells you to wait. Which part of your brain should you follow? Neither.

Set aside enough time to do justice to your message and your client's issues. If you give in to a squeezed time frame, you turn the meeting over to Murphy by letting your eagerness dictate. Your first meeting should be to confirm your reconnaissance with proper probing questions and to establish a relationship. That leads to a second meeting that becomes a solution meeting. Your agenda responsibility is to state the possibility of a next meeting so that there are no surprises on the part of your client. But remember to present the agenda in terms that relate to the client's needs, not yours. Clients will always defer to their own issues versus ours. Gear the agenda to them, and they'll follow you anywhere.

BOTTOM LINE

Whenever possible, wait beyond the first meeting to make a sale. The more time you spend with the client, the deeper the relationship and the more trust you will be given to develop solutions to the client's needs.

CREATE A CRITICAL PATH COMMITMENT

MURPHY STRIKES

I usually soar when I make a sales call. My product is great, and I love discussing it. Then comes the end of the sales call. For some reason, I choke. How do I keep the confidence?

Remember how you outlined an agenda at the beginning of the meeting that set out a road map for how the sales call would proceed? You laid out a path for the next 30 minutes to an hour, had the client understand, received an agreement, and then went ahead.

That's what you will do when you close, except the path you propose will cover several days or weeks instead of minutes. You are offering options, including the scheduling of your next steps together, to the client. Does the client agree? If not, let her point out what doesn't work with that particular part of the schedule and then come up with an alternative date or sequence of events.

Tying up a sale isn't about having the client say yes or no. It's about offering options that let the client visualize the process of becoming your customer. Constructing a critical path of commitment lets you provide a schedule of action—dates included—that begins with an agreement between your client and you and ends up with the delivery of your products and services.

A critical path means establishing certain events and time frames in a chronological order for a client. When clients see a critical path, they see implementation. They see how your recommendation actually gets realized. A critical path helps clients and begins to make your recommendation real.

A critical path also shifts the focus from a yes or no response. You're not asking for a sale. You're asking for an agreement to continue the dialogue.

> So I will have those estimates to you by Tuesday, and we will meet that Thursday at 2:00. Is that good for your schedule?

> You'll talk with your financial officer this week, and I'll meet with you again on Monday morning. How does that sound?

Summarize during the meeting, looking for clues to what the client needs to have recapped to keep him up to speed. And know when to summarize. Summarizing at the right time is an art. As a salesperson you must know when a client needs to understand what has just been covered.

Bring this tacit closure throughout the conversation to make sure the client is clear. It moves the conversation forward and keeps the meeting progressing positively. It gives you a window into the level of agreement your client has to your recommendation.

> Again, Jane, we have four new product launches next year. The lowest-priced item may not be right for your retail goals. The other three, higher-margin items may work well with your retail objectives. Am I on the right track?

Bill, am I right that you said our monthly updates that keep you informed on inventory levels at our warehouse would be helpful to you?

From summaries such as these, you can then build your close.

We determined earlier that three of the four new products might have a place in your new season. Let me work out a schematic that includes projections for the next 3-, 6-, and 12-month periods for these three and present it to you next week. How does Thursday sound?

You said that our monthly reports on inventory at our warehouse would be an asset. I will get the latest inventory reports for the products that seem to be the best match for your goals and bring them to our next meeting. Does the 16th work for you?

When you construct your close, remember to quantify the need. My wife, Ellen, has a powerful phrase that she uses in her selling efforts. She will say to a client, "Give me a nickel and I'll return a quarter to you." Do your best to quantify the benefit of your recommendation to your client in terms that are easy to understand. Breaking a recommendation down to its elemental parts is a skill.

Also let clients quantify the urgency of their need. A potential client once asked me to come in to explain my services and what I might offer her sales force. She told me that her sales force often dealt with art dealers, but her staff had difficulty getting their clients to sit down to a meeting for 30 minutes of quality time to listen to a value proposition. "Instead," she told me, "they end up selling in the dealer's showroom, with too many distractions." I jotted down what she told me in my client notes.

Being forced to make hurried sales calls in an inappropriate setting is death to sales (as my client could certainly tell you). I knew this client needed my help, but did she see it?

As I began to close, I asked her how often her salespeople get the short shrift. She told me "all the time." I asked her to count those lost sales meetings. Then I asked her to estimate how much each meeting could have brought in sales. As she began to quantify the lost opportunities, she began to see the urgency of the sales training I was recommending.

This closing was my foundation for creating a critical path that included me returning to meet with her to present a proposal that would answer the urgency and frustration that *she* spoke of during our meetings, using her exact words.

Clients will give you the reasons to follow up during the meeting. Your job is to collect those reasons. You need to determine the follow-up points that are meaningful to your unique client. You need to prioritize these points (some will be more critical to the client) and deftly use them throughout the closing. By the way, you can be sure that the proposal I designed for this client used the exact words my client used and directly spoke to her need.

STEVE BUSTS MURPHY

Trial-close your client throughout the presentation. Do it within the first 3 minutes of your presentation and then many times after that. Use questions like: "Do you see the value of this going forward?" "Can you see this helping your business?" "Any question here?" "How does this sound to this point?"

Your close at the end of your presentation will simply be the last of these closings, but at this point remember to *always articulate the next step that you will take and your client will take.* In other words: Who, what, and when.

BOTTOM LINE

Practice the close throughout the meeting. And if you must choke, do it during your practice.

RESOLVE ISSUES TO CLEAR THE CLOSE

MURPHY STRIKES

I think my presentation worked, but as I leave I'm second-guessing myself.

Closings often fail because a salesperson has not resolved certain issues to the satisfaction of the client. I have seen salespeople answer client questions flippantly, briefly, and tentatively throughout a sales call. With each missed response, Murphy adds slime. Too many missed responses guarantee a close that never sees the light of day and a Murphy triumph.

Closings fail if the client ends up closing for the salesperson. Your job as salespeople is to deliver the close, not leave it to the client (or Murphy). Even when the client articulates the close, we must process that action and determine if that action is the most fitting close. Understand the client's close and ask questions to determine your alignment with the close before you agree. You also need to make sure that there is no additional baggage to the close that could alter your expected outcome.

I always have my client notes from my probing meetings with me when I close a client. If my client says something that is new or contrary to our original issue, I quickly go back to my notes and determine where this data fits in with what we've discussed.

My notes come in handy in case there's any question of my statements. I have always carried a red marking pen. The red marking pen reminds me of key issues that needed resolving throughout my probing meetings. The specific issue that my client said was the most important pops out at me as I craft my follow-up proposal.

When I take out my red marker and write down or circle a problem issue, it tells the client, "I've heard you and I know it's important." I have a client on Wall Street who now takes my red marker from me whenever we meet and circles his issues that he wants me to resolve! During our last meeting he took my portfolio that I write my client notes in and sketched out the issues that formulated his last training session.

As you finish an aspect of your proposal, ask your client a question about it. *Listen* to the response! It will tell you whether he's on board or not. Notice the delivery of his response, enthused or tentative? Notice what his response is, clear or muddled? Both his physical delivery of the response and his content are essential for moving forward or retracing your last point. Move forward too quickly and Murphy picks up your next sentence, oops!

Think about walking across the street with a child. My sister-in-law lives in a beautiful part of rural New England across the road from a horse farm. When my nephew was a small boy, we used to walk over to the corral and visit the horses. From the moment we left my sister-in-law's home I held his hand as we crossed the street and walked along the road's edge. With each step I was always aware of his whereabouts. He was 4 years old and possessed the attention span of a 4-year-old.

Your client isn't 4 years old, but clients need to have their hands held. Their minds drift, and when they do, Murphy squeaks in. Watch clients as you close. Are they distracted or are they following you like a murder mystery? Gear your behavior accordingly.

Finally, remember that if the plan doesn't fit, you must quit. Plain and simple, making a sale that's not right is just bad business. Have the discipline to realize that it's not to everyone's advantage to make the sale. Tell the truth to your client. It's in both your interests to retreat and make another appointment to address the issues that need to be resolved. The issues may require more research either by you or the client. Never sell bad business; it will hurt you in the short run and long run, and it will also make Murphy king.

STEVE BUSTS MURPHY

Ask for your client's thoughts at the end of the meeting. Even though some clients don't want to, most people do tell you the truth. Listen. Maybe it's good; maybe it's bad. Either way, when it comes to honing your presentation skills, you need to hear honest assessments.

BOTTOM LINE

Always have the war now and peace later.

11

EVEN MURPHY KNOWS THAT WHEN IT'S OVER, IT'S NOT OVER

THE HOW AND WHY OF FOLLOW-UP

Mary, a diligent, caring magazine advertising saleswoman with whom I've worked over the years, once received a request for proposal (RFP) from an ad agency. Across the first page of the RFP, in big, bold red letters normally reserved for "Danger, Will Robinson!" types of situations, were the words

DO NOT FOLLOW UP WITH ANY PHONE CALLS

Mary, the diligent, caring saleswoman that she is, respected the client's wishes. She did not follow up with a phone call to see if she'd been selected for the business. She might as well have had Murphy on her speed dial.

Then she waited. And waited. Four weeks later at an industry event, she ran into her client. "Hey!" he said to her, "Got your proposal. How come you never called?" Taken aback, Mary said she was simply following specific instructions on the RFP. "Oh, we always put that on our proposals," the client replied, "but nobody adheres to it. I was waiting for your phone call."

Amazing, but true. It makes you want to scream, but forget the screaming. The lesson here is to always follow up! But, make sure that you follow up in a friendly, professional manner.

At the end of the first episode of the 1960s TV detective show *Colombo*, starring Peter Falk, the villain is being led away when he says to the indefatigable lieutenant, "I never met a person so persistent yet so likable in my life."

That comment perfectly sums up the ideal combination for follow-up. Despite the fact that Colombo was returning to the suspect again and again to gather more and more information that would eventually trap the culprit, the murderer nonetheless couldn't help but like him.

This, dear friends, is our mantra in the profession of sales. Nothing ever takes the place of persistence. Being persistent while maintaining a likable demeanor tells your client that you take pride in your efforts and you have respect for the client. It communicates that you expect results from this collaboration and that it is not okay with you if the business relationship you have established just dies on the vine.

I coach salespeople to kill people with kindness. Kindness is, of course, a virtue, and that alone is reason enough to practice it. But consistent kindness is also a business asset because it allows you to effectively and amiably frame your tenacity. It sweetly and sincerely communicates that you are not going away!

Kindness takes many shapes and sizes. There are hundreds of kind, smart gestures you can use to follow up with clients that are tailored to their business goals and their individual personalities. You need to discover these goals early in the process and initiate your tailored response at the appropriate time.

THE SECOND DATE STARTS ON THE FIRST

MURPHY STRIKES

After I had what I thought was a solid, fruitful sales call, I called the client to say thanks for the great meeting. Instead of a nice response, however, the client was downright rude, telling me that she really didn't have the time to be on the phone and that next time I should contact her secretary. I apologized, hung up the phone, and took the rest of the day off to lick my wounded ego. What gives with the Jekyll and Hyde routine?

Think back to when you were dating (it hasn't been that long has it?). Follow-up is a lot like that. When you finish a terrific date, you don't just say, "Thanks, had a great time!" and then hightail it. No, you say, "Thanks, I had a great time. Want to go to the movies on Saturday?" It's natural, sincere, sweet, and effectively continues your new relationship.

It's the same with selling. You must generate enthusiasm for continuing the relationship during your first encounter. You don't wait until a week after the first date to make the second one. You begin the second date before the first one is over.

Follow-up begins during the meeting itself, not after. This is critical. As you meet with your client it's important to observe and document in your notes certain follow-up actions that would be acceptable to your client.

If your client says she has a specific deadline, develop recommendations that help her meet that deadline and then use your recommendations as the springboard to meet again. If the client says he has a numerical target, then make note of the target during your sales meeting. That number should be at the center of your follow-up ("You said you needed to target more 25- to 40-year-old women and the plan I've developed can meet that goal perfectly. Would next Tuesday be good to bring it over?").

You're being kind, you're being responsive, you're being useful. And—go figure—you're getting your next meeting.

There are many reasons you can use to follow up with a client. Find and understand the reasons that are uniquely meaningful to each client before, during, and after a meeting. Prioritize them, and then use them deftly throughout the follow-up process.

While it's important to specifically tailor your follow-up to each client, there are, generally speaking, four major reasons why you should call after a meeting.

1. To check the status of your recommendation.

2. To determine why a recommendation has stalled.

3. To get feedback on a new aspect of your recommendation that will benefit the client.

4. To meet a genuine deadline agreed upon at your last meeting.

Check the status of your recommendation.

After a meeting where you have laid out a recommendation, you need to follow up to get an overall status report on where that recommendation has landed. Where has it gone? Whose desk is it sitting on? Follow your recommendation. Is it on the money trail, that is, the right path that will lead to a decision that will result in a sale? Find out.

Has your recommendation landed with someone other than the person with whom you met? *Red flag!* Why did this happen? Who slipped your football to whom? Why? Why weren't you told? (Of course, we both know that we're never told, but that shouldn't stop you from wanting to know about your recommendation—this is, after all, your baby.)

Once you discover where your recommendation sits, politely insert yourself into the trail again and establish a rapport with the person who has your decision. Retrace your selling steps. *Caution:* You might uncover the fact that you let something slip (you may have forgotten, for example, that no new purchases will be made until the next quarter) or you may find out that the client who promised to push your ideas with vigor has gotten lazy and is sitting on them instead.

Here's where humility and tenacity come in. Use these attributes effectively and you'll write Murphy out of this picture. With all your humility begin the questioning process with your contact.

Now probe. Ask your contact clear, focused questions to see the situation the way she does. Why has she treated your recommendation the way she has? Once you figure out her reasoning, you will have the facts necessary to use empathy to respectfully, but tenaciously go about altering that perspective.

As stated before, masterful salespeople have clients self-realize the next appropriate step to take. Your job is to shepherd the client clearly and quickly.

If the decision has moved on to someone else in the chain of authority, determine who is sitting on your recommendation and how that individual fits into the decision mix. Make sure you are in that mix, too, and arrange to see that person as soon as possible. ("I believe it's best if I met with the director of imports so I can explain this first hand and determine if it's right from her perspective.")

After you've made the appointment (which you did immediately, right?), prepare as if you're meeting a brand-new client. Impress the new client with your humanity and thoroughness. Achieve the decision you've sought from the beginning.

Determine why a recommendation has stalled.

There are plenty of reasons why someone might have hit the pause button on your recommendation, but there's no good reason not to find out why. Maybe the client's busy. Murphy drops in on even the most buttoned-up of us. Maybe your ideas haven't jelled well in the days following your presentation.

Whatever the reason, arrange a brief catch-up meeting with your client. Begin the meeting with three to four open-ended questions to understand his own business pressures. When I do this, I'm always amazed how quickly clients apologize for the delay and then begin to reestablish, on their own, the next steps to move the buying process along.

Sometimes the apology happens at the mere suggestion of a catch-up meeting. Regardless of the reason for the delay, get the follow-up meeting. Should there be a real problem with your recommendation moving forward ("Accounting looked at the numbers and couldn't make sense of your projected increases."), the great news is that you are face-to-face, aware, and ready to resolve the issue or retarget the next step that needs to occur to continue the buying momentum. Uncovering what needs to be strengthened lets you move forward.

Get feedback on a new aspect of your plan that will benefit the client.

One of the best reasons for follow-up is to discuss a new or additional aspect of your recommendation that brings enhanced benefit to your original idea. This is bulletproof because you are seeking feedback on an idea that will only help the client.

At the follow-up meeting, rearticulate the critical path to accepting your original recommendation. Reviewing the original recommendation is essential because the buying momentum has slowed down. Reviewing it enables you to newly stimulate your client to the benefit of accepting the recommendation. The new idea, as an addition to your original recommendation, shows your concern and ongoing creativity.

Meet a genuine deadline agreed upon at your last meeting.

A genuine deadline that you articulated during your last meeting and your client agreed to ("So, I'll call to check on the progress of this plan before you leave for the quarterly sales meeting, right?") is an important reason for follow-up. You have every right and need to get back to your client if a deadline must be met in order to provide your promised product or service to the client.

Be sure that you are empathetic when you connect with your client and that you have a solution that will solve her deadline issue. ("I'll bring six copies of the plan when we get together so you'll have enough for everyone at your meeting.")

Of course, sometimes when you call for a follow-up, the client will try to shine you on. When he comes up with a weak excuse for not seeing you, be ready. Here are a few tips for handling typical brush-offs.

I'll call you tomorrow/next week/next month/soon.

Lesson one: *Clients don't call back*. If your sales presentation ended with one of these phrases or you hear this when you follow up with a call, then you did not properly close your sales meeting. If a client says "I'll call you," then take your calendar out of your briefcase (or better yet, have it out from the beginning of the meeting) and say "Great, what day works best for you next week?" The client naturally will need to respond with a day. Respond with a smile, "Great! Morning or afternoon?"

By doing this you communicate that calling back is important to you and important to the meeting that you've just had together. The client's response also gives you insight into the level of urgency that the client has drawn from your meeting. The client may have led you to believe that she was ready to act on your recommendation, but it could be that you feel the urgency more than she does. Pin the client down to when she will be calling; it will help you discern the client's level of urgency to go forward, a desire that's key to making the sale.

Let me think about it.

Red flag! Red flag! This is a major blow off! Almost every objection in business requires that it be narrowed down (my thanks to the excellent book *Stop Telling and Start Selling* for this crucial point). This statement, whether or not you realize it, is an objection. Ask your client, "As you think about this recommendation it sounds as though I should too. Which aspect of it should we put under the microscope to discuss together?" Another response could be, "Which part isn't making sense for you? Let's discuss it now and resolve it."

This communicates a sincere request that the client explain himself. You need that explanation because, at least up to this point, he hasn't given you any indication that issues or doubts gave him the need to think further about meeting again. If there are issues and doubts, then now is the time to bring up that part of your recommendation that needs to be looked at again.

We're waiting until next quarter to make any decisions.

This statement should not come to you at the end of a presentation. If it does, then you did not ask the client the right question at the start of your meeting to understand the timeline of urgency. For example: "Henry, as you look at your current situation and as I look to tailor a solution for that situation once we've agreed on a match, when do you see implementation?"

Understand the level of readiness to proceed aspirationally at the start of your meeting versus discovering hesitance at the end of your meeting.

We're in our budget process now. I'll get back to you next month.

Once again, you need to find this out at the start of your presentation, not at the end. Flush out the client's resistance to pinpoint her anxiety or worry. Should she maintain that nothing can be decided until the budget process is over, you still need to close her on whether or not your recommendation matches her needs. Once she has agreed that your recommendation is what she needs, then you can discuss the budget process and when implementation can begin. Also, remember that budgets are flexible. Clients find budget lines for things they want. Your job is to make certain that your recommendation is indispensable.

We're going into our busiest season; the timing is off.

Maybe it is the client's busy season. Maybe it's not. So what? If your client is going into his busiest season, maybe now is the most important time for your product or service. You must maintain a certain level of alacrity throughout your relationship with your client and be the spirit of optimism and opportunity. Feel enthusiastic and show it. It's the only way the client will ever feel it.

The best way to avoid brush-offs, however, is to preempt them with probing questions at the start of a sales presentation. By doing this, you can get a sense of the level of participation and commitment your client has.

STEVE BUSTS MURPHY

Okay, so you get a follow-up meeting and you get your head bitten off and treated like a time-wasting no-goodnik.

To err is human, to forgive divine. (The client is, of course, in the role of the error maker and you, appropriately, are in the role of the divine.) Outlast your client with respect and kindness, and you'll go forward to overcome this rude interaction. All of us have bad days. She could very well be having one. Let it go.

Ask her administrative assistant how her boss's day is going before you speak with her again. Develop a relationship with the assistant now that you know you might have a tempest in a teapot. If the assistant works for a hothead, you'll probably have a sympathetic ally.

But, what if it's not a case of temperament, but something more worrisome, i.e., your performance at the last meeting? You think you had a solid, fruitful sales call, but did the client indicate this or are you just assuming so from your perspective?

Always take the temperature of your client before the meeting ends. Ask questions throughout the meeting to verify your own set of feelings. Doing this also brings forth direct feedback regarding the success of the meeting as it happens.

If you asked at the end of your meeting, "Is this direction on track to achieve your primary goal?" and she said, "Yes, once we get this up and rolling I can then initiate a stronger campaign in the fall," you could then know for sure that you and your recommendation are exactly on track. Ideally, you would send her an e-mail that same day recounting the alignment that she spoke of.

BOTTOM LINE

Don't waste the client's time. Be ready for a hotheaded reaction. Don't take it personally. Rise above your hurt feelings and concentrate on the client's goal.

CREATE A CRITICAL PATH AND TAKE IT

MURPHY STRIKES

I thought I had prepared myself to present a closing that would get me to the next step of the sales process, but every time I offered a date for my next meeting with the client, he would answer (while going through his date book), "Nope" and "Can't meet Tuesdays" and "March is looking pretty tight" and on and on. Finally he said, "When I find an opening I'll call you." I couldn't tell if he was really busy or just avoiding step two. What could I have done if he was that tied up or, worse, if he wasn't?

Throughout your selling efforts with a client always be thinking ahead to create potential critical paths. Make the process of accepting your recommendation easy for the client. Observe your client's method of making decisions—spur of the moment, indecisive, needs reassurance—as early as possible in your sales process. This will help you design a critical path for quickest acceptance.

Here's an example of a critical path:

January 11, sign proposal. February 1, arrange meeting with client company's president. February 5, phone interviews with president's meeting attendees. February 10, program delivery.

Through the use of a critical path, the follow-up's natural next steps are chronologically presented to the client at the meeting. Write them out so that your client readily understands what lies ahead. Reinforce the schedule with an e-mail that repeats it. This underscores your consistency and quietly evidences your professionalism.

Several years ago I was consulting with a bank in its corporate finance area, having been asked to decide how best to sales train its bankers. Typical of large institutions, there were several people involved in making the decisions regarding training. As one thing led to another, I noticed my recommendations for training begin to slip away as too many cooks threatened to spoil the broth.

You could almost smell the trouble brewing. Things got quiet. Uncomfortably quiet. In sales you must develop a sixth sense to feel when a sale is slipping away, but it's usually because you dropped the ball (didn't shepherd the client through the process) or real issues developed to slow down or stop the process.

You are responsible for maintaining a client's enthusiasm throughout a sale. I repeat, it's your responsibility, not theirs.

After the meeting, I made a series of phone calls and not one was returned. The specific data I had asked for at the meeting and was told I would get was not delivered. When I finally got through to these four decision makers, I could hear their tentativeness and preoccupation with other issues. I sensed that the buying fire that I had created was going out.

But, I had put too much into this to walk away. You can only imagine the level of passion and tenacity I needed in order to keep my recommendations from slipping away.

When you feel it slipping away, *get back to clients in person*. My sales instinct told me to see the whites of their eyes again to understand what was slowing down the process. Was it justified? I had to get back to them to determine the real issues that were responsible for this slowdown.

I realized that I needed to (nicely) keep myself in front of my clients, all four of them, on a consistent basis. I began a campaign of follow-up that reached each of them with training data and newsworthy articles on corporate finance that I knew matched their client base and business goals. This process lasted for 8 months.

Yes, alas, I am only a mere mortal and even I have to do battle with Murphy.

Finally, during the last week of the eighth month I made contact with my primary decision-making client. We agreed to meet the following Monday to catch up. Amazingly, my client immediately stated at the start of the meeting—before I could get my meeting agenda out of my mouth, a real rarity for me—that the bank was going ahead with the yearlong training program that I recommended due to one, overarching reason. He told me, "We're hiring you because we have never seen anyone track a client as consistently as you have with us. That's the kind of dedication and know-how we want for our bankers."

All I could think was, "Wow, this stuff really works." (No matter how often you say it or how much you think you know it, when a simple truth is proven anew it's sometimes as though it's for the very first time.) My second thought, though, was, "Boy! How many other clients did I let slip away when I wasn't this tenacious?"

Staying in front of the client—in a helpful way—highlighted the selling style that the client wanted for his bankers. Each action you take communicates much more than just the act itself to your judging client. Besides showing that

I care and I'm a professional, my actions also bespoke the sales style I knew would be the best for those bankers to follow.

Finally, your follow-up actions collectively communicate your genuine desire for business or your lack of desire for it—even when you can't get them to return your phone calls or e-mails! Remember, it's not about them. It's about you.

STEVE BUSTS MURPHY

A client simply *can't* find time in his busy calendar for a follow-up? Think about it: You're there to help his business. That makes you the exact thing his calendar should be filled with. Something's amiss here. Whether your client is truly that busy or not, the way he was flipping through his calendar indicates he had lost sight of the importance of your next meeting, meaning he had lost sight of the importance of what you had to say.

It was at that point you needed to take a step back and determine: Did he understand the urgency of the second meeting or did you not communicate the urgency clearly enough?

But, let's say he really is that busy. Find out who else can act on his behalf to continue your sales process while he's away at meetings, the sauna, seeing the Queen of England, or however else he manages to fill his workdays. Using the very same reasons the client has already articulated as essential to his overall business goals, state the importance of the second meeting as a way to reach those goals. Emphasize how a time lag will only further distance him from those goals.

On the other hand, if you realize that you're getting a disappearing act, then you need to ask him several questions to confirm what was just discussed to see if he's either changed his mind or allowed another issue to slow down the process. Either way, get at the heart of the procrastination and remove it.

BOTTOM LINE

Act with the knowledge that a follow-up meeting is essential to the client's business goals. Be sure the client understands this. If the client is truly too busy to meet with you, determine who is able to step in as an alternate decision maker.

WHO CARES?

MURPHY STRIKES

About 6 months ago, I received a pretty good response to a sales call and was told to call to set up a second appointment. Calls were avoided or excuses were made whenever I tried to follow through. Finally, last week, I called "just to check in" and the client replied, "Look, let me save you the trouble. When I have time, I'll call you. That way you don't have to keep calling and maybe that would be better for both our busy

schedules." I felt as welcome as Typhoid Mary. How did
I so misread what seemed like plain English?

Do you think Colombo cared that the suspect was fed up with
his seemingly inane questions? Hardly. Colombo continued to
ask and resolve his questions with a single-minded determination. Of course, he always did it in a nice way, and with the
murderer's acceptance!

The essential point here is forbearance, keeping yourself in
check when provoked, being patient and restrained. Sales are
not about getting angry, annoyed, insulted, or exacting
revenge. They are about kind persistence, especially in the
follow-up.

The moment you put off calling or sending that e-mail to
your client when you know you ought to, you surrender the follow-up mission to Murphy. Take a guess what he'll do with it.

Often when I was pursuing this bank, I'd say to myself,
"Oh, what's the use anyway. . . ." And each time I thought this
I'd also think, "If for no other reason, do it because you said
you'd do it." Looking back, it amazes me how much better I
felt each time I sent an e-mail or made a phone call, even
though I rarely received responses to those phone calls or e-
mails. But, each night when I left my office I could honestly
tell myself that I had done my best.

As with so many aspects of sales, to follow up correctly and
professionally *you cannot take anything personally*.

Develop nerves of steel. Never think that the client's apa-
thy is directed at you. Swarm the client with kindness and
outlast the client with concern.

Remember the following:

1. *Be persistent, yet likable.*   Strong-arming doesn't work. It might for the short sale, but for a relationship that will last 5 or 10 years it doesn't. Clients know when a sale makes good business sense. Clients enjoy being pursued providing that the pursuer isn't rude. Being likable is essential to understanding where a client is in the buying process. The client won't come clean with you if you've acted inappropriately. Persistence illustrates how much you care for your client and for having a relationship with them beyond just the sale.

2. *Kill with kindness.*   With the close of each business day you must look back at that day and determine if you did the right thing by people. Kindness requires confidence and maturity, an ability to look beyond yourself and consider others. All clients have pressures on them, some of which we know about and some of which we don't. I am not recommending that you become a client's personal valet, but you should perform kind acts for your clients to consistently show them your goodwill, even if that act is simply a sincere inquiry about their day.

3. *Be tenacious.*   There is no substitute for tenacity. Tenacity shows belief in one's self and belief in one's product. Tenacity also sets a tone of honesty, one which allows the client to tell you what's right and what's not, knowing that you will persevere to make things work out to your mutual benefit.

4. *Tailor follow-up to your client's situation and needs.* Tailored follow-up communicates caring. It says you matter to me. It says I've given a lot of thought to your unique situation. Tailored follow-up communicates how you will interact with a client as you move forward and what the client can expect of you.

5. *Have forbearance.* The definition of forbearance is patient restraint, keeping yourself in check under provocation. When you feel like telling a client, "Get off it and decide!" you instead hold back. Empathetically deal with your client. Restrain yourself, and communicate with your client in a mature, caring way. Take your time and stay on course.

6. *Outlast them with concern.* Nothing takes the place of caring for people and their business goals. You stay in love even if they fall out of it. Discipline yourself to listen first and talk second. Evidence concern. Staying concerned says, "If you need to pull back, I'm still here, I'm still concerned. When you are ready, I am too."

STEVE BUSTS MURPHY
You thought things were hunky-dory during the sales meeting, but afterwards you couldn't get arrested in the client's parking lot?

People and priorities change. Do some reconnaissance with people who surround the client to determine if the interest that was initially made was genuine and what would be the appropriate step to take to get the next meeting.

As the book *Getting to Yes* recommends, look behind the ultimatum. Begin some interviews with this executive's direct reports to pinpoint if your product is the match to them that you were led to believe it was. After those meetings, you will have a clear indication on how to proceed even if it is to go back to the beginning again.

BOTTOM LINE

Agree on the follow-up during your meeting, not afterward. If you get resistance, determine the reason then and there. As you seek to follow up, remain tenacious, but kind. Keep the client's needs as your top priority.

INDEX

ABOUT THE AUTHOR

Stephen A. Giglio is founder and president of the Giglio Company, a sales and executive coaching consultancy whose clients include American Express, Citibank, ESPN, and other high-profile corporations. An award-winning sales professional in his own right, Giglio and his firm have helped thousands of sales professionals around the globe hone their selling skills and instincts.